HOMESPUN

"*Homespun* reads like a leisurely visit with an old friend. It starts off with light, chatty topics before settling into the-deep-part-of-the-heart experiences, such as a young mom recovering from the stillborn birth of her little boy. At times charming and humorous, at other times profound and heavy, this collection of true stories will linger in your mind long after you close the book."

—SUZANNE WOODS FISHER, BESTSELLING AUTHOR OF *AMISH PEACE*

"Real voices of Anabaptist women—from traditions as diverse as Old Order Amish to car-driving Mennonites—open up about faith, family, hopes and dreams, and experiencing life's trials and joys with God by their sides. As a man who is not Amish or Mennonite, I was not sure how this book would resonate with me. I have to say that it did. The women's testimonies here are frank, vulnerable, funny, powerful, and often profoundly moving."

—ERIK WESNER, FOUNDER OF THE WEBSITE AMISH AMERICA

"The short pieces in *Homespun*, as diverse as the women who wrote them, focus on issues central to the lives of Amish and conservative Mennonite women, including childbirth, cooking, in-laws, dating, mission work, home decoration, marriage, and above all, friendship. All the chapters evidence a profound

Christian faith that makes *Homespun* a collection that will delight and challenge readers."

—KAREN JOHNSON-WEINER, AUTHOR OF *TRAIN UP A CHILD: OLD ORDER AMISH AND MENNONITE SCHOOLS*

"Filled with wisdom, humor, and hard-won faith, *Homespun* feels like a lovely visit with trusted friends. A must-read for those who wish to better understand the lives and hearts of Amish and Mennonite women."

—SERENA B. MILLER, AUTHOR OF AN *UNCOMMON GRACE*

"Talented Amish and Mennonite women bare their souls in words that evoke a whole range of human emotions. They were not all born with a wooden spoon in their hands, and they experience the same struggles as women everywhere. It was impossible to do anything else until I finished reading this book."

—ROMAINE STAUFFER, AUTHOR OF *LOYALTY TEST*

HOMESPUN

AMISH AND MENNONITE WOMEN
IN THEIR OWN WORDS

LORILEE CRAKER
editor

HERALD
P R E S S

Harrisonburg, Virginia

Herald Press
PO Box 866, Harrisonburg, Virginia 22803
www.HeraldPress.com

Library of Congress Cataloging-in-Publication Data
Names: Craker, Lorilee, editor.
Title: Homespun : Amish and Mennonite women in their own words / Lorilee
   Craker, editor.
Description: Harrisonburg : Herald Press, 2018. | Includes bibliographical
   references.
Identifiers: LCCN 2018007805| ISBN 9781513803289 (pbk. : alk. paper) | ISBN
   9781513803289 (hardcover : alk. paper)
Subjects: LCSH: Mennonite women--Religious life--United States. | Mennonite
   women--United States--Biography. | Amish women--Religious life--United States.
   | Amish women--United States--Biography.
Classification: LCC BX8128.W64 H66 2018 | DDC 289.7/73082--dc23 LC record
   available at https://lccn.loc.gov/2018007805

Most chapters in *Homespun* first appeared in one of the following publications and appear here with permission of the editors and the writers:
   Ladies' Journal is a bimonthly magazine published by Ladies' Journal, PO Box 138, Loysville, PA 17047. Subscription information available at 717-789-3288. *Daughters of Promise* is a quarterly magazine produced by Anabaptist women and distributed both digitally and in print. Subscription information available at daughters-of-promise.org or PO Box 189, South Boston, VA 24592.
   "Bone Opp-a-Deet!" by Linda Byler first appeared in the October 2017 issue of *The Connection* and is used here with permission.
   "Overcoming Inferiority" adapted from *Overcoming Inferiority* by Sara Nolt. ©2016 Christian Light Publications, Inc. Harrisonburg, VA. Used by permission.

Scripture quotations marked (ESV) are from the ESV® Bible (*The Holy Bible, English Standard Version®*), © 2001 by Crossway, a publishing ministry of Good News Publishers. Used by permission. All rights reserved.
   Scripture quotations marked (NIV) are taken from the *Holy Bible, New International Version®, NIV®.* © 1973, 1978, 1984, 2011 by Biblica, Inc.™ Used by permission of Zondervan. All rights reserved worldwide. www.zondervan.com The "NIV" and "New International Version" are trademarks registered in the United States Patent and Trademark Office by Biblica, Inc.™
   Scripture quotations marked (KJV) are from the *King James Version*.

HOMESPUN
© 2018 by Herald Press, Harrisonburg, Virginia 22803. 800-245-7894.
   All rights reserved.
Library of Congress Control Number: 2018007805
International Standard Book Number: 978-1-5138-0328-9 (paperback);
   978-1-5138-0328-9 (hardcover); 978-1-5138-0317-3 (ebook)
Printed in United States of America
Cover and interior design by Merrill Miller
Cover and interior photos by Lana Whetzel, La Bella Luce Co.

22 21 20 19 18   10 9 8 7 6 5 4 3 2 1

Contents

Introduction

I'm just a simple Mennonite girl from the prairies.

This is what I tell people, and it's true. As a two-week-old adopted infant, I was brought to the home of my Mennonite parents, Abe and Linda Reimer, on a slushy April day in 1968. From that moment on, I was their daughter, grafted into the family tree and over four hundred years of Mennonite history.

On my mom's side, we are country folk, descendants of Mennonite pioneers who traveled from Ukraine in the 1870s, carrying scoops of hearty winter wheat from the Old Country to plant in the new. The Loewens and the Brandts of Rosenort, Manitoba, still speak Low German (*Plattdeutsch*) and partake of *Faspa* (a late afternoon lunch) on any given Sunday. The ties of language, food, and culture that bind them to their pioneer great-great-grandparents are startlingly durable. The Isaacs and Abrams and Sarahs and Lydias of old, who lugged steamer trunks halfway across Canada on Red River carts and abided in sod huts, would be so proud.

My dad was born in 1937, in a Mennonite colony in Ukraine. He was born into a holocaust waged by Stalin against his own people. By the time my dad was ten months old, he had lost his twin sister, Anna, to starvation. At age six, he fled with thousands of other refugees across Ukraine by foot, fleeing Stalin. He arrived by boat in Canada in 1947, a ten-year-old immigrant Mennonite boy.

You see, I knew from early on that there were lots of different kinds of Mennonite stories.

But I didn't know until I went away to college in Chicago at the age of nineteen that there was anything peculiar about being Mennonite. Hey, in Winnipeg, Manitoba, where I was raised, you can't throw a *Fleisch Perishky* (meat bun) without beaming another Menno on the head. Upon arrival in Chicago, I quickly realized, much to my surprise, that most people outside of Mennonite communities assumed I had come from buggy-driving, bonnet-wearing, butter-churning folk. Everyone seemed to think that being Amish or Old Order Mennonite and being *my* kind of Mennonite were one and the same.

This assumption led to lots of explanations on my part about the difference between my modern Mennonite upbringing ("like Baptist, with a German accent and special foods") and those other related subcultures. It also led to me writing a whole book about the Amish, who I came to realize were more closely tied to me and my upbringing than I had ever dreamed.

As I visited Amish homes and barns in Michigan and Pennsylvania for my 2011 book, *Money Secrets of the Amish*, I recognized bits of their dialect, *Deitsch* (Pennsylvania German), from my spotty grasp of Low German. The Amish women's hair buns and long skirts, not to mention the tantalizing aromas of fruit strudels (*Platz*, to me) baking in their ovens, reminded me of my beloved grandma Loewen. I recalled my little dynamo of an *Oma* (grandmother) tsk-tsk-ing me about the length of my skirt. She always had a twinkle in her eye as she chided me, but I still made sure to go for full coverage as I interviewed the Amish.

Among the Amish, there was a feeling of welcome, of peace and simplicity. I felt oddly at home among my spiritual and cultural cousins. Both Amish and Mennonites are Anabaptists, a Christian group that began during the 1500s and continues in a variety of forms today.

These combined elements in my background prepared me well to curate this book you hold in your hands. I was excited to cross those hospitable Anabaptist thresholds again, if only through the writers' words. I knew I would find a gentle spirit in the writings of my Mennonite and Amish sisters, and I was right.

Even though some of these writers drive cars and hold jobs like the rest of us in the world, their rootedness in their Anabaptist heritage sets them apart from that world. In these writings, most of which are drawn from two Anabaptist women's periodicals (*Daughters of Promise* and *Ladies' Journal*), I found a sisterhood of women with shared values. As I read dozens of essays and devotional pieces and true stories, all written by women, some themes arose.

Welcome. A deep sense of hospitality is fundamental to these women. Yet it's not hospitality in the HGTV, your-house-needs-to-be-perfect kind of way. "It is easy to overthink hosting," writes Vicki Kauffman. "There's no formula for the perfect menu, the perfect conversation, the perfect music playlist. Our Lord Jesus made it look quite simple, and his hosting style can be described in one word: love."

Abide. Hospitality is sacred and spiritual, but it doesn't mean these writers don't want to have an appealing home space in which to dwell. They want to abide in an abode, if you will, that nurtures them and feeds their spirit. "Keep it simple but significant," says Bethany Hege in "White Space." The writers here expound beautifully on what home means to them.

Testimony. Stories make the world go round. When we hear the stories—the testimonies—of others, we are better able to understand our own story and our place in the world. These narratives stirred different emotions in me. My heart ached for Ervina Yoder as she described what it was like for her to be the mother of a longed-for but stillborn baby: "I go grocery shopping and no one knows I'm a mommy," she writes, from a to-the-bone level of honesty. I was inspired and encouraged by Danielle Beiler's trust in God as her provider: "If God owns the cattle on a thousand hills, he can take care of my needs." And I giggled at Mary Yoder's secondhand testimony of an Amish man whose pants were just too stretchy. Poor guy was definitely in a "ferhoodled" state of mind!

Wonder. The blazing faith of early Anabaptists is evident in the openness of these writers to all things wondrous. This short-but-sweet section easily could have been filed under "Testimony," as the four pieces are true stories of miracles, phenomenal happenings that don't make sense from a human perspective. But these tales deserve their own section, as they highlight the possibility of the miraculous happening all around us, in big ways and small.

Kindred. A core value of both Mennonites and Amish is the preeminence of family—kinfolk, whether they be kindred or not. I grew up with dozens of cousins between two close-knit families, and I thought that's how it was for everyone. Our kin shape us in ways both known and unknown, good and bad. These essays and stories speak to the tremendous influence of family, from our great-grandparents to our children. Writing about family trees, Gertrude Slabach offers this pearl of wisdom: "Whether we're part of the tree from our beginning or whether we were grafted in, we belong. We not only belong to the tree; the tree is a part of us. Those knots and gnarled limbs? There's a story behind them."

Beloved. As I sifted through these essays, I was struck by the faith shining through. More than once, tears came to my eyes, and I lay down the piece I was reading to meditate on it a bit. These essays enthused my soul, and I came away feeling as if I had just been to church. My cup had been filled. There is something wonderfully elemental and childlike about the devotion expressed here, devotion even in doubt. These pieces drew me closer to the One who calls all his daughters "beloved."

In closing, my wish for you as you read these *wunderful gut* pieces of writing is that you will enjoy them as much as I did. You don't have to be a simple Mennonite girl from the prairies to do so. All you need to do is open your heart and let the homespun words of these women enlarge your worldview, extend your heart, and increase your friendship with the Creator of all good and *gut* things.

—*Lorilee Craker*

1 WELCOME

*W*hen I think about my growing-up years, I remember all the company we would have to our
humble bungalow on Kingsford Avenue. Guests would
often eat on trays in the living room, because our little
kitchen could hold no more than six or seven around
the table. I also remember visiting Mennonite family
members, and almost always their greeting to us at the
door was "Welcome!" (or "Velcome!" with a German accent). The word was always said more than once, as if the
speakers wanted to doubly and triply convey their heart's
wish: that we would feel invited and wanted, and that we
would know that we belonged there with them.

As I chose the pieces for this book, a strong theme of
hospitality emerged in the words of these openhearted
writers, and I was challenged anew to rethink my concept of welcome. I love the words of Rae Schrock in her
piece "Love Begins in the Kitchen": "Don't fail to invite

friends to gather around your dinner table because the space is small and the chairs will fit awkwardly. Instead, happily offer what you have, knowing that the largeness of your kindness balances the smallness of your home."

"True hospitality," says Gertrude Slabach, "is about blessing others with belonging, value, and importance." In other words, it's more about your guests than it is about you.

These words pierced my proud heart as I thought about my beautiful patio set, almost unused this summer because of my anxiety over "too many weeds" in our yard. I had made hospitality about me and my imperfect space, rather than about whom I could bless with an open heart.

Whom can you and I bless with acceptance in this season? To whom can we extend a grace-filled welcome?

Lovee

~ *1* ~

Love Begins
in the Kitchen

RAE SCHROCK

*T*he way I feel about my house is largely defined by how I feel about my kitchen. Love begins in the kitchen, because food begins there. And food, as we know, is the gem around which we gather to experience some of our most meaningful interactions. It is important to me that the area of my home associated with rich fellowship be worthy of it.

When I lived at home in Tennessee, the kitchen and dining room were always full of laughter and loud voices. My family has spent dozens of hours lingering around the dinner table, talking. Meals are our time to be together. I think it's safe to say we spent more time all together in the kitchen than anywhere else in the whole house. The pale green walls have seen hundreds of guests come and go, as Mom stirred love into every pot of soup and kneaded generosity into each loaf of bread. Around the delicious food we have gathered with family, friends, and even enemies. Around food we have learned about friendship and the value of those around us. Some of my most treasured memories took place in the warm, savory air of our home kitchen. I bet yours have too.

Since I moved away, things have changed a bit. I cook less frequently and certainly less extravagantly, because for most meals, it is just me. Guests don't come and go the way they do back home, and there is definitely less noise: two things I miss quite a lot. Now I have set about trying to carry on my mother's legacy of hospitality. I enjoy people, and inviting guests into my home is high on my list of priorities.

My apartment is quite small, however, with very little storage area, and my kitchen is no exception. Maximizing the tiny space has proven to be a challenge, but also great fun, and I have learned a few things along the way.

One of the first things I noticed about the kitchen on my initial tour was the drawer situation. There are only two.

I also discovered that it is impossible to fully open one of those drawers without first opening the oven door. And when it came time to find a home for my vast array of kitchen utensils, I ran into a problem: I have way more stuff than will ever fit into two measly drawers—especially one that doesn't open all the way!

So I got creative. I bought a lovely red crock and stuffed most of the vast array into it. The rest of the lot I hung on a four-by-four-inch pegboard I purchased for about eight dollars and painted bright red. It hangs in my very tiny dining room, which adjoins the kitchen.

An old beat-up bread box serves as my "junk drawer": a place to store screws, extra lightbulbs, garden seeds, lighters, and other odds and ends.

The cupboard situation is not quite as dire. Still, I have been forced to flex my creative muscles a bit to fit it all in. I'm a serving dish junkie and have amassed quite a collection. After a lot of shifting and rearranging, I finally got all my cool dishes to fit. I bought racks so I could have two-story levels in the taller cupboards, demonstrating that it is indeed possible to stack serving bowls seven high.

I'm also a huge fan of varied spices, and again, have quite a collection. To free up cupboard space, and because I can't stand the domino effect that happens when you reach into the second row of spice jars, I found an alternative. Baby food jars, meet the back of the stove.

Months ago, I relieved a friend of about twenty empty baby food jars. They gathered dust for a while until I remembered I had them and retrieved them to upcycle into spice jars. A little Goo Gone took care of the sticky labels, and some chalkboard paint over the lids created the perfect erasable canvas for marking the contents of each jar. I bought spices in bulk (to be thrifty, of course), loaded up the jars, and lined the back of the stove with them. It saves drawer space and looks awesome too.

It's been helpful to think of my kitchen in terms of vertical rather than horizontal space. Shelves and pegboards are a fun and effective solution for using open wall space. Small stands or tables with shelves have also been essential in expanding my limited counter space and storage areas. By using them, I can double or even triple the available room in my kitchen.

My good friend Gertrude bought me a swanky green-shelved table, which I use to hold my espresso machine and all my baking canisters. Voilà! Last summer I ripped apart an old pallet and made a nifty rustic table that now holds the microwave, my wine-bottle tiki torches, and utensils arranged in attractive containers. There is also room beneath to store the mixer, along with a plethora of vintage strainers and pitchers stashed in a primitive egg basket.

When you use vertical space, there is endless possibility. Simple crates, baskets, or decorative boxes stacked together provide lots of extra storage without giving the kitchen a tacky, disorganized feel.

Extra surface area can be found on the top of the fridge also. Set an old crate on its side for an attractive way to store your collection of cookbooks or small houseplants. Hide cereal boxes behind it—they don't fit well into cupboards.

One of the lessons I learned from my friends in Brooklyn, who fearlessly and frequently host large groups, is to offer generously what you have. Don't fail to invite friends to gather around your dinner table because the space is small and the chairs will fit awkwardly. Instead, happily offer what you have, knowing that the largeness of your kindness balances the smallness of your home.

My own apartment kitchen is much too small to realistically hold more than six or so people at a time. So I have turned a lot of my energy to the large space I do have: my backyard. Making it an inviting, colorful space gives me the flexibility to invite as many people as I want. We can all fit in the yard and have a merry time too! Last week a whole crowd of local friends came over for an ice cream party and outdoor movie in my backyard. It was phenomenal—a perfect solution to my tiny indoor entertaining options.

I must also put in a good word about stocking a kitchen on a budget. I'm a hard-core thrifter, and almost 100 percent of the items in my cupboards are secondhand. It is entirely possible to have a wonderfully unique kitchen on a budget. I love plain white dishware. It is simple and can be used for formal and casual dining. Did you know the dollar store sells it? Okay, so maybe the dishes aren't made to last for twenty-five years. But you can't beat the down-to-earth simplicity of a simple white plate that's a little scuffed or even chipped.

One of my favorite parts of my kitchen stock is the silver-ware. A lover of diversity and pizzazz, I will never in my life put plain metal silverware on my gift registry. Instead, I've been slowly collecting plastic-handled silverware. Some of the pieces are new, some are cheap, some are vintage. It's so much fun to eat with this stuff! It is colorful, unique, and vivacious, and at only a fraction of normal cost.

I urge you to get creative with your kitchen and dining pur-chases: upcycle, shop at thrift stores, or build your own. It is sat-isfying to have a cost-efficient living space that is also uniquely you. Remember this: the fellowship and friendship shared over a good meal (even if it's just takeout pizza) begins in the kitchen. Keep this space tidy and accessible, making creative use of however much or little area you have to work with. In the end, guests will appreciate most the love of a well-lived-in, orderly, and inviting space.

Rachel

~ 2 ~

An Unforgettable Lesson
in Hospitality

SARA NOLT

*M*y mind was whirling as I picked at my food at the ladies' brunch and listened to a teaching on biblical hospitality.

"The Bible talks about entertaining strangers..." The speaker told how God had given her family a way to host strangers. She read an impressive list of countries that had been represented in their home in the past year. Even guests from "hard-to-reach-with-the-gospel" countries had been in their living room!

I love other cultures and countries. I wanted to witness to people from around the world in my living room too. But I hadn't even known it was possible in our rural Plain community. In other words, I was jealous.

As soon as it was convenient, we invited this speaker's family over for pizza. We were kind. They were kind. And then we hit them with The Big Questions that ran out of our mouths faster than we could phrase them intelligently: "You host people in your homes from all over the world and we want to do that too, and is there any way we can, and how can we get involved, and is there a place for us, and how soon can we get started . . ."

We came up for breath at last and let them talk. They told us about the University of Delaware and its program that teaches English to people from around the world. Often, students who study abroad become leaders in their home countries, which multiplies the potential of a Christian witness exponentially.

One popular option for the international students is a program in which they have contact with a host family at least once a month. The students love it because they get to visit American homes, where they are immersed in American culture and get to practice their English.

Were we interested? Of course we were interested!

"Come with us to a meet-and-greet," our new friend told us. "There you'll meet students who want hosts, as well as the coordinator for the program."

That was the evening we joined the program as hosts. Within a month we had Seung, a South Korean, playing croquet in our backyard.

When we signed up for the program, however, I was worried. We aren't exactly a typical American family. Our guest students weren't going to have tailgate parties at ballgames or Fourth of July fireworks or Christmas trees. Or television.

What fun were we going to be? Would they even like us?

Those fears were thoroughly laid to rest that very first evening. After the meet-and-greet, our friends took us with them to visit a veteran host family who lived in Maryland.

I think half my questions were answered the minute we pulled into the driveway of their home. I had worried that our home was too ordinary to host rich students from Saudi Arabia who talk about honeymoons that include three different countries plus a cruise.

But the home we entered rivaled ours for simplicity. It was tiny. The exterior was simple, unfinished, and had no landscaping at all. There were children everywhere. That meant the entryway doubled as the boys' bedroom. Leaving the bedroom-entryway, we entered the living room, where construction was obviously underway, for the floor was unadorned plywood and the ceiling was attic.

I walked into a tiny kitchen where the Queen of the Home was at work. There were open cupboards with potential for countertops, but there were no countertops. And no sink. And no faucet.

Wait. How can you have a kitchen without kitchen essentials? She was smiling and stirring something on the stove. She was used to it. She also appeared used to the furnace in the corner and the pile of tiles beside it.

"So how long have you been working on your home?" I asked.

"Ever since we moved here eight years ago," she said matter-of-factly. "We used to have a sink in the kitchen, but it just drained into a bucket that we had to carry outside to empty."

I tried to discreetly scrape my jaw off my knee as I mentally did the math. Here was a woman who, in this tiny house, had obviously birthed babies, raised children, and hosted hundreds of people from around the world. All while living in a perpetual construction zone.

The food was ready and resting on the table in the living room. We adults sat on the few pieces of living room furniture, while children and plates carpeted the floor and our hosts started talking. They talked nonstop about their experiences with hosting international students and of the incredible opportunities they encountered.

"I was in my bedroom on my knees pleading with God to give us an opportunity to share the gospel when I heard my young son take a Bible storybook over to our student," our hostess said. "My son started talking about the stories in the book, and my husband used the moment to witness . . ."

I forgot about the house. I barely noticed the ruckus the children created when they zipped in and out and around the house, with ice cream trailing behind them.

Our hosts talked for hours. They told about getting invitations to visit former students now back in home countries across the world. The woman spoke of praying for the money needed for tickets so she and the baby could travel alone to northern Africa, where a student was alone in her faith and begging her to come.

Their students obviously loved them. They didn't just come to their home once and leave for good. They came again and again and brought their friends along.

I was challenged. Inspired.

It grew late. I picked up dishes that still sat on the table-turned-buffet. I wanted to be helpful. But where do you go with dirty plates when there is no sink, counter, or water in the kitchen?

"Oh, take them into the bathroom."

Yes. The bathroom. Of course.

With my armload of dishes, I crossed the living room and passed the girls' room—a rectangle barely large enough for two beds and other bare essentials. I passed the door to the only other room in the house, the master bedroom, then used my foot to open the door of the bathroom. On my right were the toilet and bathtub. To my left was a washing machine, topped with a tea towel and piled with clean dishes. In front of me stood a lone laundry sink. The open door ate up the floor space.

I deposited my armload of dishes among the ones already nestled deeply in the sink. I would have washed them. I wanted to wash them. But I felt helpless in this tiny bathroom, with its singular sink loaded with dirty dishes and no counter. This woman was incredible.

When we left shortly thereafter, I carried with me the greatest lesson in hospitality I have ever been given. It isn't your home that creates the atmosphere to draw guests to return. It isn't beautiful decor, tasteful paint jobs, or inspirational wall words.

It is the presence of Christ and his love within you that draw the strangers and cause them to return.

Sara

A Life That Says Welcome

VICKI KAUFFMAN

Home: a topic romanticized by poets, artists, and songwriters. A place of safety and intimacy, of familial camaraderie, of healthy relationships and spiritual and emotional moorings. Home is the sharing of life with people you love, in both the mess and the beauty. As Laura Ingalls Wilder said, "*Home* is the nicest word there is."

Rome wasn't built in a day, and neither are our homes. They are the intricate layers of trust, respect, and intimacy that take time to develop and build. When these sacred building blocks are violated or absent, the result is a home held up by pain and hurt—a virtual and emotional prison for its inhabitants. The power and concept of home lie not in the walls and doors, however well decorated and gorgeous they may be, but in the spirit and atmosphere they contain.

Part of our calling as ladies is making our homes comfortable and enjoyable for others. And since home is more than a building, our beautifying goes beyond the decorating of walls and the arranging of furniture. Our thought processes will not be limited to paint colors and style but will include personal development, growth, the formation and beautifying of the soul, and the discipline of being at rest in God. A woman with the wild joy in her heart of being God's—and who has learned how to rest and be satisfied in him—will adorn her home in ways that couches and mirrors cannot.

Welcoming people into our lives and into our homes will automatically follow in a life that belongs to the simple carpenter from Nazareth. Interestingly, Jesus had no home—no beautiful physical place in which to invite guests over. I don't think people missed that, though, because they had his presence, and into that he invited them. They flocked to him to be cared for, healed, forgiven, accepted, and loved. As his daughters, we too carry this holy privilege: that of loving and serving others. Inviting them into our homes is one of the noblest things we can do for Christ.

Our guests should be as varied as the spices in our cabinets, and the way we interact with them as varied as the way we use our spices. If you have friends from different cultures, you will understand that friendship has different definitions wherever you go. Latin cultures tend to be warm and friendly; my Hispanic friend makes herself at home in my kitchen, washing the dishes and searching the refrigerator for what she needs. When she comes over, I try to leave some food prep for when she gets here so that we can work and laugh and enjoy each other. Her involvement is beneficial for both of us. She is comfortable and at ease because our cultures are temporarily integrated, and I have the benefit of watching guacamole and tacos get made the way they were meant to be made. We both win, because we both are comfortable.

My blue-haired, tattooed, and pierced friend who comes over sometimes is more guarded, and I have to work harder to understand her. Our interests and values are vastly different, so finding common ground takes patience, wisdom, and tact. I enjoy her honesty and her questions, and I feel the liberty in our friendship to reciprocate by asking her questions as well. We both represent minorities—subcultures in a greater culture—and while our lifestyles are polar opposites, we understand what it feels like to not fit in to our greater culture. We are a study in contrasts, my friend and I, but our friendship is special to both of us.

When my conservative Pentecostal friends or my church friends come over, the conversations feel effortless, because of so many shared values and similarities in culture, lifestyles, and goals. These are the easiest friendships to have and maintain, and they are the ones we go to in crisis. Because they are easy, we often end up in these friendships by default, and we have to work harder to achieve the same results with people who are different from us. However, to only invite people into our homes and lives who are like us is like cooking only with salt and pepper. The flavor profile begins there, but it only becomes interesting with the smoked paprika, the garam masala, and the chili powder. We need to intentionally build friendships with those who will add to our lives in ways that will round us out. These friendships make us bigger people, and through them God's kingdom can be expanded.

Inviting people into our homes and lives is one of the most challenging but rewarding things we can do. As people have come through my home and sat on my couch, and as I've been in friends' homes and sat on their couches, I've learned a few things.

The need to be valued and respected is one of the most basic needs of the human heart, one that Jesus filled in every person with whom he interacted. When our guests sense the same authentic, heartfelt interest, they will feel welcome and at home with us. Cultural and religious walls will begin to crumble, opening up space for ministry and opportunity.

We live in a lonely world. Although we are incredibly connected through social media, the number of lonely people is higher than ever. The number of people with no support group and nobody to call in a crisis is astounding. As Christians, we should be aware of these needs, and we should move in intentional ways to meet them. Listening well and asking good questions are sometimes the best things we can do for our guests. And when the emotional bucket is dumped, we need to give people the gift of privacy and not pass on information to others. Our homes should be safe places to talk and be heard, and gossip infringes on these needs for privacy. Some people feel very connected through gossip and the passing on of hurtful information. If that is what makes us feel comfortable and connected, then we need to seek Jesus' face and ask him to show us what really matters to him and let that change us.

A restful and relaxed spirit is one of the most beautiful qualities of someone who hosts. This restfulness is a learned and trained virtue, as Mary demonstrates in the Scriptures when she sits at the feet of Jesus. It is hard to enjoy your guests and listen and interact in meaningful ways when you're running around, worrying that everything is perfect. The truth is, most of us don't feel comfortable with perfect, so we hold a double standard in hosting and being hosted. There is no perfect clutter-to-clean ratio that we should try to achieve, but being real about our homes and lives is actually a beautiful gift to our guests. True friendship and intimacy mean enjoying the reality that life is both messy and beautiful.

Being a gracious receiver will also invite guests into your life in ways that will make them want to stay. Friendship is a two-way street, and if you are unwilling to let your guests help when they offer, or if you shrug off a sincere compliment, you make it difficult for your guests to love you the way you are trying to love them. Graciously accept the compliment with a simple "Thank you, I'm glad you enjoyed it." Accept the offer to help with the dishes or sweep the floor. This makes it easy for them to reciprocate your love in the best ways they know how.

* * *

While inviting people to share your life and home largely has to do with your presence and spirit, it is also practical. Here are a few tips for creating a setting of welcome.

Be intentional about decor. A globe or world map is a timeless decorating accessory that says you care about more than yourself and your own little world. These items are great conversation starters and can get interesting discussions going. And instead of using a traditional guestbook, start a gratitude wall and get your guests to write their blessings on color-coordinated sticky notes and hang them on your wall. This creates a unique wall display and highlights the variety of your guests.

Prepare for each guest individually. Tailor your hosting to accommodate each one. My newly married friend loves to cook delicious, nourishing meals for me when I come over, because she remembers what it's like to work all day and come home tired and hungry. She also sends leftovers home for me to enjoy later. This simple gesture makes me feel incredibly loved and welcome in her life. Incorporate these little things into your hosting and serving.

Be intentional about conversation. Be prepared to ask questions and start topics of conversation that everyone can enjoy and contribute to. Avoid conversations that only a few around your table can be a part of. In a big group, the quieter ones can easily blend into the woodwork. Be proactive about including them in conversation and activities.

It is easy to overthink hosting. There's no formula for the perfect menu, the perfect conversation, the perfect music play-list. Our Lord Jesus made it look quite simple, and his hosting style can be described in one word: love. When we love human-ity with his love, our homes won't be able to hide it. His pres-ence will be felt, which is ultimately what it's all about.

Welcoming well isn't so much about doing the right things; it's about being. By *being* secured and fulfilled in Christ, our *do-ing* will flow naturally and beautifully. People will feel welcome and at home in this life-giving and serving kind of love. And in a strange and wonderful way, as we offer it to others, we get to grow, change, and experience life more fully too.

Vicki

~ 4 ~

On Appreciative
Overnight Guests

LINDA BYLER

*O*ur house has two large guest rooms, which are enough to bring on a sense of melancholy. Five daughters, all married and with homes of their own, have left my upstairs with a dubious collection of odd-looking furniture, heirloom quilts, and old vases with white plastic roses. Those sweet plaques about motherhood that hung on the wall for their allotted time? They are now squirreled away with the other objects I cherish but do not want in the living room, dining room, or anywhere else. Not even the bathroom.

Last summer one of our daughters and her family, who live nearby, were taking their turn hosting the church service. Our oldest daughter, who lives eleven miles away in another district, decided that she and her family would come for the weekend so that they could attend church at her sister's house. Now, eleven miles might not seem that far away. But it's quite a stretch by horse and buggy, especially in warm weather. So this resulted in a phone call: "Mom, we're coming for the night."

This happens so seldom, and we were thrilled to have daughter Laura, son-in-law John, and the boys come overnight on Saturday and for breakfast the following morning.

So humming and whirling, plying the T-shirt dust rag and my trusty microfiber dust mop, I prepared the two rooms with anticipation. Laura and John have four boys, so we'd put all the boys in one room: two in the double bed and two on piles of quilts, blankets, and comforters.

We'd put Laura and John in the other guest room, which with its many items from the taxidermist, appears to be designed for a person who loves to hunt and buy old furniture. A black bear climbs out of the wall, complete with a faux rock, and a sad-eyed buck with resplendent antlers faces him from the opposite wall. (I'm sure the buck had a sense of foreboding, thus the sad expression.) There's a magnificent Canada goose with outspread wings, decoys, and hand-carved shore birds—well, you get the picture. In this room there is also a bed that has a firm mattress of questionable lineage, bought at a secondhand shop before all the flap about bedbugs.

I got clean sheets, pillowcases, and battery lamps, and fixed the blinds in the windows. Everyone should enjoy a good night's sleep, I thought to myself as I made the beds.

My daughter Laura is a wonderful cook, whereas I do the best I can with the pathetic amount of culinary skills the good Lord has given me. But anyway, I try. I whipped together an "overnight in the fridge" breakfast casserole with the same panache with which I prepared the guest rooms. Whirling and twirling, pinkie extended, I whistled under my breath. Such wondrous hospitality!

Laura's family arrived after a meal at the local diner, so the huge box of potato chips was forgotten, as were the dips and the brewed sweet tea. Still, we enjoyed our evening immensely, sans prepared snack. We all went to bed, with loving "Good nights." My husband and I rested well, woke up the next morning refreshed, dressed ourselves in our Sunday best, made a pot of coffee, and waited eagerly for the family's appearance.

* * *

John and Laura came down the stairs together first, with pale, drawn faces and the distinctive red-rimmed eyes that speak of very little sleep.

"Did you sleep well?" I chirped, pushing back the absolute knowledge that they had not.

"Mom, what in the world is up with your acorns?"

Acorns? Oh yes. The acorns that fall from the gigantic white oak tree in the front yard. Those acorns. Right.

"We hardly slept. *Bang. Roll, roll, roll. Plink!* All. Night. Long." My daughter groaned. "And the traffic! Just when I thought I could fall asleep there'd be a roaring sound, accompanied by a vivid display of lights on the ceiling and walls. *Zoom. Zoom.* Then the traffic would stop awhile, and we'd be back to the acorns. *Thump. Roll, roll, roll. Plink!*"

"And where did you find a mattress as hard as that one?" she asked. "It's like sleeping on a board!"

The rest of us laughed at her description of the miserable night. I poured cups of coffee, and we discussed the artillery-like sounds of the acorns also hitting the metal roof of the barn in the backyard. We laughed some more. When you have outspoken daughters, nothing is hidden for the sake of being polite.

We sat down to eat, and I served the breakfast casserole. Soon Micah, the picky eater, spoke up. "This is sick!" he said.

His mother was horrified and tried to fix the situation. But it was all right. I'm used to frank comments about my food, and we laughed about that as well.

Soon we were walking down the hill to church. The familiar sound of steel-rimmed buggy wheels and iron-clad horses' hooves approached us and passed, and the slow-moving vehicle emblems on the backs of the buggies flashed in the sun.

As we walked, I thought of how accustomed we become to the way things are, and the way that the obvious can escape us. My husband and I are so used to acorns attacking in the fall that we don't even notice them. And personally, I think that firm mattress is wonderful. I slept on it for years.

So all was well. I swallowed the tiny bit of pride that remained after raising seven children. John and Laura went home to their own bed that evening, likely with huge sighs of relief and thankful hearts that they live back on a long driveway, away from traffic, and with nary an acorn in sight.

We're supposed to *herrberg gerny*: a Pennsylvania German term that means "be generous in hospitality." I certainly was. I was pious, devout, and well meaning. True, I did send our guests to bed with bombarding acorns, roaring traffic, mattresses like plywood, and a breakfast casserole that *was* a bit heavily salted, come to think of it.

But it is a night that will be repeated many times. Everyone is already enjoying a good laugh about it. Hopefully it'll never be lost among the many humorous stories of our family's history.

Linda

Open House

GERTRUDE SLABACH

*T*here's somebody pounding on the door," my friend Sandy told me. (Names have been changed.)

It was two o'clock in the morning. Who could it be?

The night seemed foreboding. Could this be a ploy? Looking through the window, I saw a woman, crying, on our porch. "Please help me. I've been raped," she sobbed.

Cold and trembling, she rushed inside when I opened the door and ushered her to the sofa. In short gasps, she told her story, admitting she had lied. She had not actually been raped, but she was indeed scared. A man had offered her a ride home from the bar where they had met. Instead, he drove down the forlorn river road. When he threatened her, she opened the car door and fell out. Waiting in the bushes until she thought he was gone, she ran to my trailer, which is nestled next to a large warehouse by the river.

"I saw the light on the porch, and I felt I could trust you," she said.

The man had driven by and then turned around, coming back our way. That was when she begged to be let inside. Even after she was inside, he kept driving by our trailer.

In addition to Sandy, there were two others in our trailer that night. My sister was asleep in the room we shared. An elderly Amish man was asleep in what used to be my bedroom.

When it seemed safe to leave, we drove the woman to her apartment. We never saw her again.

Was it wise to allow her into our home? Is it wrong to take such risks? Do we only invite others into our world when we feel prepared and safe?

Lying in bed that night, wide awake after we had taken her home, I remembered my prayer from a few months before. As a single woman working as a nurse and living with my sister fifty miles away from our home, I had been feeling disconnected. Plus, I was frustrated that my schedule prohibited me from participating regularly in church events. So one day I told God, "I feel useless, with little to give, but I offer my trailer to you."

God took me up on that offer. Within a few months, a family had asked permission to park their motor home at our place during the father's hospitalization. They hooked their power to our electric meter and ran a hose from our water supply. Several weeks later, Sandy, a single mom, had asked to stay with us one night a week while taking college classes. Our sofa became her bed. During that same period, an Amish woman from our community had surgery at the hospital where I worked. We offered my bed to her husband, Reuben, and I moved into my sister's bedroom. That was why both Sandy and Reuben were with us the night this woman arrived on our porch.

I thought all I had was a two-bedroom trailer.

* * *

God only asks us to share what we have. He will use it. When the disciples suggested that the crowds be sent away, Jesus instructed them to feed those people. Really? Feed five thousand men plus women and children? They had been busy all day long. It was late. They were tired and wanted to go home. Then again, should hospitality only be practiced when it looks fun?

In the midst of this was a lad with a lunch of five loaves and two fish. It was not much, but it became more than enough.

God asks us to share what we have for his use. On a whim one Sunday, my Sunday school teacher invited her class for lunch. I have no idea how more than a dozen boys and girls squeezed into her family's car for the ride home, and I cannot tell you what food was served or the design on the plates at her table. All I know is that, fifty years later, this is still one of my favorite childhood memories. What made it so special? Her spontaneous warmth and affirmation.

God will use what we willingly share. The Shunammite woman saw Elisha's need as he came through her community (see 2 Kings 4). She and her husband built a simple room onto their house with a bed, a table, and a chair. Her purpose? To meet the needs of the prophet. What an example of gracious hospitality!

God will use what we have and share. When I was a child, my church owned three meetinghouses, one centrally located and the other two at opposite ends of the county in which we lived. Our congregation rotated worship services between the buildings, meeting centrally one Sunday and at opposite ends of the county on alternate Sundays. Because of the travel distance, those of us from outside the community in which a particular service was held would simply choose homes to visit for lunch, arriving unannounced and uninvited. What fun to decide where we would go that Sunday! On alternating Sundays, *we* were the ones waiting expectantly to see which guests might come to visit us. Years later, my aunt described the one Sunday that people kept coming, and coming, until she had twenty guests plus her family of eight to serve.

We have lost something since then. Perhaps some of us never found it in the first place!

Hospitality is an art and a command. Some of us might need a little more practice and experience, but the ability is right there if only we are willing to hone that heart attitude.

When folks feel the warmth and welcome of a gracious host, they fail to notice a less-than-perfect house. Lonely people need belonging and care, not exotic food and fanfare. Waiting until we are "ready" or until we "feel like" having company is no way to practice hospitality. In fact, it is not true hospitality.

True hospitality is about blessing others with belonging, value, and importance. Hospitality is the affirmation we give to others that they are worthy.

When we invite folks whose lifestyles we cannot approve of into our homes, we are giving them Jesus. When we share what we have to help ease the burdens of others, we are sharing the compassion of Jesus. When we provide rest and refreshment for God's people, we are enabling their mission.

God wants us to give what we have, willingly and cheerfully. He wants us to open not only the doors of our homes, but the doors of our hearts as well.

gertrude

~ *6* ~

A Side of Conversation

RAE SCHROCK

*S*haring meals together, whether with family or friends, invites us to do something that is difficult in our modern age: slow down and enjoy our food and each other. For a few moments in the midst of racing lives, we can come together and relax. We can share laughter and sorrows, facts and ideas. The table is an emblem of community; gathering around it, we have the opportunity to nourish our souls as well as our bodies. Eating together is a rich tradition of the Anabaptist community, and one we must pass on to preserve.

I was raised in a large Anabaptist family by parents who placed a high value on shared meals. We often hosted visitors, and our dining room drew the company of newcomers and old friends alike. Some of the most heated conversations of my life have happened around our honey-brown table, as well as some of the most healing ones. As an independent adult, I've shared meals with comrades all around the world, lingering long after the meal to discuss the richest stuff of life. Leaving those gatherings, I feel full, both physically and emotionally.

Latin American and Spanish cultures place such a high priority on interaction shared at a common table that it even has a name: *sobremesa*. The term literally means "over the table," but it carries a deeper meaning that doesn't translate to English very well. One website defines the practice as "the time spent after we finish eating, before getting up from the table. Time dedicated to chatting, socializing a bit more, digesting our food, nourishing our souls. We stay at the table as long as we possibly can. No meal is a complete one without a long *sobremesa*. In Spain, how we eat our food is as important as what we eat."

In Western culture, many families are fragmented at mealtime. Supper is a bag of fast food inhaled on the way to soccer practice, or a prepackaged meal consumed on the couch. Starved for time, our culture steals extra minutes wherever possible, and mealtime is often the first to be robbed. Why go to the work of cooking a meal, assembling the family, and cleaning up the dishes when we could just give everyone a TV dinner and scatter?

Consider this perspective, offered by author Michael Pollan: "The shared meal elevates eating from a mechanical process of fueling the body to a ritual of family and community, from the mere animal biology to an act of culture." I agree with Pollan. What promotes calorie-consuming to a "ritual of family and community" is the relational conversation that surfaces around the shared table. The *sobremesa*. We come together to feed not only our bodies but also our minds and hearts. Whether in the company of good friends or perfect strangers, conversation is the hub around which our interaction turns.

Conversation is as endangered a species as the communal meal, threatened with extinction if we don't work to preserve it. Anabaptists place high priority on good food, and we must make an effort to assign equal value to verbal aptitude. Being a good conversation facilitator takes practice and is not unlike preparing a meal with complementary flavors and textures. We guide with questions, good listening, and interesting contributions to create a meaningful space where guests feel valued and free to share.

* * *

My Anabaptist background gives me an appreciation for shared meals, but the skill of conversation is one I am still cultivating. Here are some tips that have helped me, and they may also equip you to facilitate conversation at your next gathering.

Be an air traffic controller, not the pilot. At your table are seated a myriad of personalities, perhaps including but not limited to Under-the-Table Texter, Can-of-Worms Opener, Silent Wall of Mystery, Hostage Negotiator, and Knowledge Bank. Each is flying his or her ideas at a unique speed, velocity, and altitude. It's not your job to take over the flight deck, dominate conversation, or have the last word. Instead, be like an air traffic controller: direct the flights of conversation with good questions and good listening so that everyone gets a chance to share. Draw connections between what people are saying, helping them explore ideas together rather than setting up camp on their own.

Welcome conflict. A good facilitator is not intimidated by heated discussion but rather recognizes it as an opportunity for iron to sharpen iron (see Proverbs 27:17). I recall one Thanksgiving dinner when a diverse mix of guests gathered around our family table and the conversation ended up in the volatile territory of racism, government dependence, and white privilege. I remember shrinking into my chair as blunt and somewhat shocking opinions ping-ponged across the table. Then I realized that nobody was actually mad at each other;

we just had intense opinions, which were rooted in personal experience. As we shared those experiences, we learned from one another and gained new tools for thinking about the issues. This wouldn't have happened if my parents had quickly shut down the conversation. So the next time you are the host and a heated issue comes up, stifle the urge to steer people to shallower topics. Shallow talk diverts conflict, but it also stifles the passion that motivates important change. Unless the debate is disintegrating into hurtful word battles or pointless argument, let it continue. In fact, consider inviting a few guests that you know are antagonists! The discussion is sure to be spirited.

Be curious. People can teach us amazing things if we take the time to engage them. Move beyond the weather to the meatier stuff of people's lives. For instance, ask "What are you enjoying/learning/thinking about in your life currently?" Curiosity is different from nosiness and is often the spark behind a meaningful discussion.

Cultivate your interests. A few years ago I noticed that at shared meals, I had little to say. My life at the time wasn't a repository of interesting tidbits; it felt boring. Others had great stories from their community interactions, deep thoughts from books they were reading, or pools of knowledge from which to share. I realized that interesting people lead to interesting conversation—the kind I enjoy most. I also realized that one doesn't become an interesting person by accident. It happens by learning about and engaging in the world around you. Since then, I've been on a mission to add interest to my life. I do this by reading books in a wide variety of genres, keeping moderately abreast of world news, and talking to people. I also have an ardent affection for podcasts. With a well-rounded base of interests and knowledge to draw from, I now find that conversation flows more organically and feels enriching.

Sometimes, mealtime with friends or family won't be all that dynamic. That's okay. Conversation doesn't always have to be riveting to be good. Sometimes the group needs light chatter; other times it wants heavy philosophical discussion. If your guests leave your table knowing that they were loved and welcome, you have succeeded.

Slowing down and savoring life together over a shared meal is a ritual to treasure. It's one so special it deserves a name: *sobremesa*. Let's work to make it an ordinary ritual of life, the absence of which would make our day feel incomplete. By cultivating the skill of conversation, we preserve and pass on this special gift: rich community found around a common table.

Rachel

11 Abide

The words abide *and* abode *are from the same linguistic roots; to me, they both point toward home. We abide in Jesus. We live and move and have our beings in our true Home. Meanwhile, here on this old blue marble, the word* home *has many evocations for people. Home is supposed to be a haven, a sanctuary where we feel we belong. The essays in this section speak to what it means to keep a home, to have a home, and even to look forward to our future, perfect home in heaven.*

Here is a different focus from hospitality, as the writers explore how various women experience home. Holli Nisly has feathered her nest with colors and furnishings that tell a very personal story. "When people come to your house, they should see who you are as a person. When people come to our house, they can easily see that I like books, coffee, and art—an excellent start to knowing me. All my thoughts can be summarized in this statement often attributed to Coco Chanel: 'Beauty begins the moment you decide to be yourself.'" Amen, Coco! (And Holli.)

One of my favorite pieces in this book is called "White Space" by Bethany Hege. She elegantly describes the soul-nourishing benefits of white space, or blank space, both in decor and in our spiritual lives. "Growing up in an Anabaptist culture with a lot of emphasis on simplicity and necessity heightened my fascination with the idea of white space," she writes. "It's easy to be enamored by something fancy or elaborate. But to find beauty in something plain and simple requires a sense of contentedness."

And in a completely different interpretation of home, Rhoda Yoder abides in the past, in a brick and mortar farmhouse she never visited but knows well all the same.

~ 7 ~

Holli's House

HOLLI NISLY

*T*he paint can said "Peacock Blue." Working the lid off, I looked around my living room. What in the world would it look like blue? I had no idea. My fears doubled when the lid finally popped off and I saw the color. Some blues hedge; they slink around with tints of green or gray. But not this blue!

Cinching my bandana tighter, effectively shutting off blood flow to my inner critic, I began. Mom and I started covering the modest mocha walls with party-hearty blue. After the second coat, I stepped back to assess the damage . . . and I absolutely loved it.

My fiancé, Brandon, on the other hand, merely commented, "That's really blue. Looks like a boy's bedroom." And that is when I decided that no matter what people said, the blue was staying, because I loved it.

This story illustrates a point about choosing colors for your house: pick colors you like. Fads change fast and often, and one thing I don't have time for is making sure I have the latest and greatest shade of color in my house.

Although I insisted on the blue, "advice sought me," so to speak, on our bedroom colors. I had decided, thanks to a lack of inspiration, that black and red would be great for the bedroom. My sister Rani, upon hearing those dolorous color choices, suggested cream and gold as something fresh and light and beautiful. I took her advice, and it looks lovely! The room is small enough that black and red would have made it look like some gloomy little hole. Cream and gold, on the other hand, fill the room with light and make it look roomier than it actually is. So when inspiration fails, ask for advice on a room. But don't ask too many people, because everyone has a different opinion.

Basically, when picking colors, I thought about three things.

1. What colors do I look good in? I want my rooms to complement me. I know jewel tones look the best on me, so while I don't wear them much, my walls do, most dutifully.

2. I also thought about the mood of the room. For instance, I didn't want to paint my kitchen anything less than cheery, because I'm not a morning person. Gray walls would only make my day worse. So as I glare at my first cup of coffee, Butter Yellow walls beam down.

3. Also, I live in Kansas. In fall and winter, brown and gray dominate the landscape. To fight the winter blues, I wanted rich, vibrant colors.

As for furniture, I found everything but our bed at second-hand stores, garage sales, and antique stores. It takes perseverance to scrounge good deals, but it's worth it! The orange and cream chair in the living room was three dollars at a junk store. The couch in the living room was free, discovered just down the road from our house. As an added bonus, it was just the color I wanted. As I furnished my house, I realized that I didn't actually need that much money to get the look I wanted. Instead of buying all new furniture, I took some time and found some really striking pieces that added character and whimsy.

The art in my house is also a story of foraging and improvisation. The three poster boards above the couch are basically glorified scrapbooking. As I attempted to organize some things one day, I realized what a hideous pack rat I was. I had boxes and folders full of pictures, notes from high school, and, well, just stuff, you know? So I bought three poster boards, arranged my scraps on them, glued them nice and tight, then framed them and put them up! The other pictures hail from the Salvation Army, garage sales, and Hobby Lobby. Foraging is a fun, inexpensive way to fill your walls with beauty, imperfect as it may be.

Which leads to the last subject: working with the flaws of your house instead of resenting them. Soon after we got married and settled in, I spotted a hole in the hardwood floor. One night, exploring an abandoned property, I found a little piece of tin with writing on it. I took it home and Brandon pounded it over the hole in the hardwood. Unusual solution, but a great conversation piece. My blah black coffee table benefited from my ministrations, and it now sports gold stripes and a checkerboard. I bought a trunk that was just plain boring, but after a day of doodling with my Sharpies, it was far from dull.

One of the more difficult fixes was the kitchen. The walls were yellow, but the backsplash was tan and red. Not a good combo. The counters didn't help matters. Brandon suggested replacing the backsplash. We did, and it made a huge difference! The counters still don't match, but it's not nearly as obvious.

Plus, we had a great time doing the backsplash together. (Just kidding. Remodeling projects are not bonding times, in our experience.)

My general advice for house painting and decorating is this: go with what matches you, not the latest fad. And if you honestly, truly don't know what your style is, grab a decorating magazine, flip through it, and see what catches your eye. Don't just throw burlap and lace together and expect it to look stylish.

When people come to your house, they should see who you are as a person. When people come to our house, they can easily see that I like books, coffee, and art—an excellent start to knowing me. All my thoughts can be summarized in this statement often attributed to Coco Chanel: "Beauty begins the moment you decide to be yourself."

Holli

~ *8* ~

White Space

Bethany Hege

*W*hen I was planning our wedding a couple of years ago, I quickly became overwhelmed by the endless color schemes and decor ideas to choose from. I wanted to have a nice, beautiful wedding, but I knew I didn't want a lot of fuss and stress over needing everything to be perfect.

I came across a quotation in the middle of the planning process that changed the course of my thinking—and not just then, but ever since. And I strive to implement it in every area of my life.

Keep it simple but significant.

I recounted this quotation often in my months of wedding planning, to remember that things don't have to be perfect or extravagant to be beautiful. This different way of thinking gave me permission to indulge in my simple, conservative inclinations without the guilt of feeling cheap or inferior. And I realize more and more the value of refraining from extravagance and abundance, how it encourages creativity and originality.

Although I didn't know to label it as such initially, this idea of significant simplicity can also be called *white space.*

White space is a term used by designers to define the blank area around an element in a design. It can be as simple as the space between paragraphs in an article, or as elaborate as a room that is white from floor to ceiling. The purpose of this concept is to pay tribute to what is important or in focus by accentuating it with a lack of anything else.

Designers use white space when creating graphics, when designing websites, in certain types of photography, and in interior design. Creating a clean image or area free of distracting elements is pleasing to the viewer, makes websites more user friendly, and states a clear purpose. Upscale brands use white space in marketing their products or services, because this simple, intentional design carries an air of sophistication and high quality.

This type of intentional design also doesn't cry for attention through the use of flashy colors and complex designs; instead, designs that use white space gain serious consideration because of the absence of those things. There's something dramatic yet calming about simplicity and the lack of clutter.

This concept isn't always popular, however. For example, a completely white room can be perceived as cold and stiff, and people sometimes simply prefer bright, colorful graphics or designs over plain and simple monochromatic ones. But there are beneficial aspects of using white space in our lives, both physically and psychologically.

Growing up in an Anabaptist culture with a lot of emphasis on simplicity and necessity heightened my fascination with the idea of white space. It's easy to be enamored by something fancy or elaborate. But to find beauty in something plain and simple requires a sense of contentedness and often a deliberate resolve to find beauty in everything around you. There is a special peace and fulfillment I achieve when I choose to be satisfied with the things I have and the circumstances in which

I find myself—even if it means living in a rural community in a house with bare walls and sparsely populated rooms. I gain the liberty to live and dream and be creative with what I do have, without being overwhelmed by things I don't need or like.

White space is often thought of in the physical or visual sense, but we can apply the concept spiritually and emotionally in our everyday lives. We can, and need, to set aside time throughout our days to pause and reflect, most importantly, on God and his Word. Our schedules might be filled with church, ministry, and outreach activities, but if we don't take the time to seek God about what he wants to accomplish in our lives and the lives of the people we're serving, our commitments become aimless.

Think of white space as the aisles in a grocery store. How difficult would it be to navigate a store if the aisles were narrow and the shelves stuffed haphazardly with items overflowing into the aisle? Obviously it wouldn't be a pleasant experience. Now think of God as the white space. If we crowd our planners with good activities but don't invest adequate time in our relationship with our Creator, we'll become frustrated and unhappy with ourselves and others.

So I'm here to give you permission (and urge you!) to stop and look around—to evaluate your grocery aisles, so to speak. God's purpose for us is that we would first seek and honor him with our lives so that we can better share his love and message with those around us. He invites us to bask in the white space in our lives—physically, spiritually, and emotionally—and to seek contentment through him wherever we find ourselves.

Clear out the clutter in your home and in your heart so you can have room to grow, change, and improve your life and purposefully serve where God has placed you.

Bethany

~ 9 ~

Where Your Soul Belongs

DeLora Neuschwander

*W*hat do you envision when you think of home? The town where you were born? The building you return to at night after work? Wherever Mom and Dad live?

Depending on what stage you are at in life, home could mean a lot of different things. Over the years, the idea of home has brought different connotations, emotions, and desires to my mind and heart. There is so much wrapped up in the idea of home that is far more than a building, color schemes, furniture, or the pictures on the wall. Home is really more a state of being in which we feel that we belong, where we are accepted no matter what, and where our souls can rest.

When I was young, my family traveled with a prison ministry. Home oscillated between a bus parked in a Walmart parking lot and a little house on Chicago Avenue in Goshen, Indiana. We were homeschooled, and most of the kids at the church we attended went to the same Christian school, so I often felt like an outsider. Although I treasure the memories we made together as a family, I realize that my identity and my concept of home were wrapped up in that life: the ministry, the bus, our travel schedule, and our music. In essence, that was where my soul felt that it belonged.

When my family decided to scale back on traveling, this sense of belonging began to slip away from me. Things were definitely changing in life, and I was once again trying to figure out where exactly I belonged. I vividly remember one Christmas when my family took the train to Oregon to visit my dad's family for the holidays. It was wonderful. We weren't at our house, but it felt like home. Everyone was loud and things were crazy, but I belonged and I was loved.

In my first semester of college, I was once again plunged into a totally foreign world, which led to a few very rough months. Here I was, the little homeschooled Mennonite girl who had no idea how to be a music major! I definitely didn't feel that I belonged, and I couldn't wait until the end of the day when I could hibernate in my basement bedroom. Thankfully, life got better, and by the end of my sophomore year, things were different. I had finally found my place. I had friends who loved and accepted me, and my heart found so much rest in that knowledge. I felt that God had healed many wounds and was finally giving me a sense of belonging.

Then God told me I needed to give it up. I transferred to a university in Ohio in the fall semester of my junior year. I think that was one of the hardest things I have ever done. Leaving the family and community I had been able to build at my old school and transferring to a new school were incredibly difficult. Looking back, I now know I was at the place I was supposed to be. But I never really and completely felt that I belonged.

* * *

Fast-forward a year, and my life changed once again. I was moving from my parents' house in Indiana, and my new home was waiting. In 2014 I signed up with a mission organization and committed to living for a year in Israel and then moving to New York to work with Jewish people. I remember lying in bed one of those first mornings in Jerusalem, realizing that life was never going to be the same. I was going to have to figure out how to make this new place home. It was an amazing year, but I knew I was there for a season and that soon I'd be starting a new life in New York.

After returning from Israel, I spent a month with my family in Goshen, and it was great. My mom cooked food for me, and I got to reconnect with my church and visit all my favorite old spots. But I was so ready to get to New York. Finally, after seven long years of waiting to live in the city, I was in my apartment and life was really starting. After so many years of packing and moving and lugging suitcases from place to place, I was finally home.

Then reality set in. Here I was, indefinitely. For the first time in years I didn't have plans to move anywhere else. I was homesick. These feelings caught me so off guard because I had never been "that person"—the one who never left home. I was always the person wanting to go off on adventures and criticizing people who had no desire to leave their communities. Yet here I was, bursting into tears of homesickness at the littlest provocation. Let's just say that God taught me a lot through that season of my life! I learned that it is okay to be homesick. We need to allow ourselves those feelings and give ourselves time to grieve those losses. Having those emotions is so special, actually, because it means we have been blessed with precious things and people!

Now, here I am. I currently live in Brooklyn, New York, with a roommate. I love walking down my street, visiting the little Russian store on the corner, and climbing up our crooked little staircase. Yes, I even love Reepicheep, the mouse who occasionally comes to visit. But once again God is dealing with me. Even though my heart is at rest in the home I am finding in this city, I am struggling with health issues. When I'm not feeling well, Indiana still seems like home. I miss my family, my people, someone to take care of me. I still don't have this all figured out.

Your journey will not look the same as mine, but you've probably had the same feelings. How do we rise above the things we feel? How do we find contentment in new situations and environments when everything inside us just wants to go home? How do we make a place home?

When you are living in a new place, it's best to get out into the community early on and keep busy. But don't beat yourself up if you don't find your place right away. It takes a while to build deep friendships, so keep trying! We were made for relationships. Sequestering yourself in your house with no human interaction often gives your mind far too much freedom to dwell on negative thoughts and emotions. Don't focus on what you have left behind, but embrace all the new things that you have been given! Go exploring and look at the changes in your life as a new and exciting adventure and not a tragic life event.

Despite the feelings that come, we must above all else cling to Jesus—daily! Not just with vague prayers before we go to sleep, but by turning to him moment by moment when those unsettled and lonely feelings come. Read Jesus' words and dwell on his promises. Memorize Scripture. We belong to God. We are his daughters, and he is our Father.

Through my journey I have come to the conclusion that home is the place where we feel that we belong. And we belong to Jesus. So wherever Jesus calls us to be, and no matter how we are feeling, right where he is—that is home.

DeLon

~ 10 ~

The Home Place

LOVINA EICHER

*T*he dictionary says home is "the place where one lives permanently, especially as a member of a family or household." Home is where memories are created. Home is a place where family can gather for comfort.

I grew up in Indiana on a farm with my parents, two brothers, and five sisters. My father was a carpenter by trade but also took care of our farm. We had milk cows that were milked by hand. Our milk was put in big stainless steel milk cans. They were kept in a tank of cold, cold water until the milk truck came to pick the milk up. Our windmill pumped the cold water to the tank.

In the summer months lots of hay was mowed, raked, and put up in our barn. Our family worked hard together to keep everything going that goes with running a farm. Loads of manure were hauled out to the fields with our workhorses. My favorites were the Belgian team Bonnie and Bell. Although scattering the manure on the field with the manure spreader was a stinky job, I enjoyed driving the team of horses. The big open fields and the peacefulness: this was my home!

I couldn't imagine the day that this farm wouldn't be my home. If I ever get married, I thought, the farm will still be my parents' home, and I will always be able to come back.

* * *

The years flew by, and at age twenty-two, I married Joe. Joe was twenty-four, and we tried to buy a few properties close to my parents' house, but it never seemed to work out. Joe and I lived with my parents that first year, and we were blessed with a precious little baby girl after eleven months of marriage. We decided to buy a trailer home and move it to a wooded area across the driveway from my parents' house. Although our trailer was just across the driveway, moving all my belongings out of the house I was born in and had lived all my life was still hard.

Time went on, and we were blessed with another daughter. That spring we found a suitable property two miles away. I was happy to have a house instead of a trailer to live in, but leaving the home place still took some getting used to. I wasn't far away and could go home to visit often.

At least once a week I would go home to my parents' house for the day. Joe would harness the horse and hitch it to the open buggy. Before his driver came to pick him up to go to work at five thirty in the morning, Joe would help me get our children into the buggy. Then I would start out. When we arrived, Mother would get breakfast for all of us, and often my other sisters would come home for the day as well. After this day at my parents' house, I found that the rest of the week would fly by and I would have more energy to do my work.

More children came along. It became harder to spend a day at my parents' house, especially once the girls started going to school, but I could still go home whenever I wanted.

Then right before we had our fifth child, my father passed away unexpectedly. Mother was heartbroken to not have Father with her. Parting was hard, but we have hopes of someday reuniting in the kingdom of heaven. Our hearts ached, and we helped Mother all we could. The last cow was sold, and their last buggy horse died from West Nile fever. The big farm seemed empty without my father, but it was still home!

We had two more children, giving us a total of six children—four girls and two boys. When our little Joseph was eight weeks old, my mother passed away. This was only two short years after Father died. Mother was only sixty-six when she died, and Father was sixty-nine.

Before long the home place was sold to someone outside the family. It hurt to not have my parents living anymore, and it was also hard not to be able to go back to the home we always knew.

* * *

Joe and I finally decided we needed a change in life. We packed our belongings and made the move to Michigan. Our new community welcomed us as we tried to adjust to new surroundings. Joe's father had moved to this community several years earlier to be closer to several of Joe's sisters, who also live here. It also helped that my sisters Verena and Susan made the move with us. Several months later my sister Emma, her husband, Jacob, and their four children also bought property in this community.

We soon felt that this place was home to us. We were blessed with two more children, making a total of eight. Life was busy! We sometimes go back to Indiana to visit family who still live there, but we are always glad to come back to our home in Michigan.

Years have gone by, and now two of our daughters have married and moved to homes of their own. They come home often. Now our home has become the home place for them! My best moments are when the whole family is gathered to eat around the big dining room table.

We do not know how long God will give each of us, but we try to live lives that please our heavenly Father. Life takes us to unexpected places, but love brings us home! May God always guide and bless our homes, no matter where they might be.

Lovina

Should You Happen to Stop By

MARTHA BEILER

There is something so invigorating about fresh spring mornings, when the birds are busily singing praises to their Maker and the sun comes up so bright and clear! Such mornings always give me a fresh burst of energy, driving me to work as fast as I can while enjoying the privilege of good health. What a blessing!

The busy spring rush is here for farmers. The list seems endless through May and June, but God always provides a way somehow. Each day we need to decide what is most important and tackle that, leaving everything else for another time.

We did a lot of double-cropping this year. My husband, Mervin, sowed cover crops—such as rye, triticale, and barley—in the cornfields after we harvested the corn last fall. These will be ready to harvest in May, plus the alfalfa fields will be ready for haying too, weather permitting. So should you happen to stop by I'll probably be out and about, either working in the barn, raking hay in the fields, or milking cows while Mervin finishes his day's work in the fields. Or maybe, if it's raining, I'll be indoors trying to catch up with household duties—or perhaps even catching a snooze, after too many late nights!

A timesaver for me is having handy foods in the cellar and freezer, because during haymaking time, I often need to slap a meal together in ten minutes. So if I know we'll be making hay on certain days, I'll cook extra food and freeze it. Baking bread and cookies and freezing them comes in handy as well.

What fun to send the children outdoors these days without coats and caps. It sure makes it easier! It's good for them to roam the great outdoors and enjoy life using their creative imagination while playing.

Already the schools are closing their doors for the summer and the scholars get to be home every day. Michael Arlin, who is six years old, will love that. It's truly amazing how much he learned in his first year at school. He loves to entertain the little ones by reading to them.

May also means yard sale month! Ask my husband or my family and they will tell you how I absolutely love yard sales. Mervin says I get "yard sale fever" in the spring worse than he gets "buck fever" in the fall. I do enjoy going to housing developments when they are having yard sales. It's so much fun to walk from house to house finding all kinds of goodies!

We all enjoyed Sam and sister Nancy's wedding at our place in February. We had a cow freshen that morning. The crowd of people didn't seem to bother her, and she delivered a healthy bull calf. So as the wedding continued, Mervin quickly changed into work clothes and took care of his farmer duties.

Last week I gave Steven (age four) and Benji (age three) Mervin's old cowboy hats to play with. They were simply delighted! It made for quite a handsome picture, two little guys with those black cowboy hats that are way too big for them! Little Kathleen, who is one, also wanted one. One of the boys' straw hats did the trick, and she was proud of wearing a hat as well. She is full of mischief! I'm quickly learning that when all is quiet, I'd better go see what she is into.

As a mother, I must teach my children a lot of things, but the greatest of these is love! I've been pondering this lately. What a beautiful world we live in, when people show love. That is something we as parents need to teach by example more than by words. Surely our children notice how we deal with other people, or what we say about our ministers or a teacher. They notice what we say about other members of our church, and about the child with disabilities who lives down the street, or the neighbors who are poor and can't afford any extras.

That reminds me of the saying "Real love is when you help someone for Jesus' sake who can never return the favor." It is my longing to teach my children the good virtues that make this life worth living. Do my children see me practice love in my everyday life?

May we love each other as God loves us!

Martha

~ *12* ~

My Father's Amish
Home

RHODA YODER

On August 18, 1930, Levi R. and Tillie M. (Schmucker) Hochstetler welcomed their firstborn son with blue eyes into their home. There would follow thirteen more sons (ten living) and three daughters. They named the firstborn son Melvin. Years later, I would have the privilege of calling him Dad.

Over my growing-up years, I heard many stories from bygone days, as my dad was an avid storyteller. Since he is turning eighty-four-years-old this year, I thought it a fitting tribute to write about his life and some of the memories he shared.

My dad was born and raised in Nappanee, Indiana. Those were Depression years, so it was a struggle for Grandpa and Grandma to make ends meet and provide for their large family. In my dad's earliest memories, his family lived on a farm with a long lane. Dad's brother Elmer, who was one year younger than Dad, liked to run out this long lane while my dad ran out a back field lane, which took him to a big pile of stones. Grandma used to say she would look outside to see two blond-haired little boys running in different directions!

Later they moved to a larger farm at the south end of the Amish settlement. Dad was old enough to start going to school while living there. But he would have been the only Amish child in a large consolidated school, so he went to live with his Hochstetler grandparents. From there he could go to school with his uncle Sol and aunt Malinda. They were only a few years older than he was. At this time, of course, the Amish parochial schools were still a thing in the future, and Amish children in that area went to public schools.

That winter Dad became very sick with pneumonia and missed a lot of school. Antibiotics were not yet developed, which meant pneumonia was a very serious illness. With his grandmother's tender care, he finally recovered and returned to school near the end of the term. Because he missed so much of that important first grade, however, reading and spelling never came as easily for him as they might have otherwise.

In June 1937, a devastating hail-and-wind storm passed through the area, causing much damage. Dad's family lost nearly all their crops. Since it was a rented farm, they still had to pay cash rent to the landowner, as well as pay the hired man. All of this left them poorer still. Dad's grandfather, John D. Hochstetler, then bought a farm close to his own home for Dad's parents, and they moved onto it in the spring of 1938. After the school term was over, Dad moved home again and went to school with his siblings for the following terms. They lived more than a mile from the school, and had a lot of cold snowy walks through the winter months.

The house on that farm was a very old large brick house with no insulation. It was so hard to heat in the winter that Grandma would put on a coat and scarf on the coldest days to go to the kitchen and cook the meals. The food was then served in the living room, where the family sat around the heating stove to eat. They also put mattresses on the living room floor. Here the children slept, because it was too cold to go upstairs.

* * *

One summer evening, Dad and his brothers were playing baseball before supper. This is something they did a lot in their spare time as youngsters, and as they got older the Hochstetler boys were noted for their expert skills in sports, including baseball. Well, Grandpa called out to them to close the gate, as he wanted to let the cows out to pasture. As boys will do sometimes, they kept on playing and forgot to close the gate. After they were in bed, Grandpa came and woke them to help chase cows back to where they belonged. Another lesson learned!

Chores for the younger boys included carrying wood and coal into the house to keep the stoves going. As soon as they were old enough, they learned to milk by hand. Later on they used milkers.

It was also the boys' job to feed the sheep. When the sheep were pastured in the orchard behind the house, Dad and his brothers sometimes had to go chase them back because there weren't any fences there to keep them in. Elmer and Dad used to climb up into an old apple tree and tease the sheep buck by throwing stones down at him. As each stone came down toward him, he would jump upward and bump the stone aside. As they got older and a little braver, they started chasing the sheep buck. He came after them, and around and around the tree they went, until the boys tired of the game. Then, quick as a wink, they climbed the tree. There they had to wait till Mr. Sheep grew tired of waiting for them and wandered away. Then they had to run for the house lest the sheep buck chase them again.

Grandpa used to plant several acres each of potatoes, tomatoes, and cucumbers. This made plenty of work for his family of boys. He paid them one cent per hamper for picked tomatoes and two cents per hamper for cucumbers. One season Dad earned fourteen dollars. That year he felt richly rewarded for all the hard work and backaches. They also had to hoe thistles in the cornfields, but they did not get paid for that.

As Dad and his brothers became old enough, they did a lot of hunting, fishing, trapping, and ice-skating, along with their ball playing. With only three girls in the family, the boys also learned to help in the house.

The food that found its way to the table in those days was simple fare. Of course, Dad's family had a large garden for fresh eating and also canning. Dishes that appeared often at the supper table were corn bread (to be eaten with fruit and milk), rivvel soup (dumpling soup), cold bread, and fruit soup or hot bread soup, depending on the season.

Navy beans were bought in hundred-pound bags. Usually one of these would last Dad's family through the winter. At a bakery in town they could also buy day-old basket bread. They would take a hundred-pound cloth feed bag to the bakery and fill it up with bread. The cost for a whole bag full was anywhere from twenty-five to fifty cents. Potatoes from the patch were also a staple. Usually, around sixty bushels were stored in the basement to last from one harvest to the next.

There were no indoor bathrooms in those days. At their house you could get cold water from a faucet, though, as they had a supply tank in a little room just off the kitchen, with a sink for handwashing. It even had a drain so the dirty water didn't need to be carried out. The water was pumped into the supply tank by a windmill. If there wasn't any wind, the boys could take turns pumping by hand. In some homes all the water had to be carried indoors, and every drop back out again.

Raising fruit and keeping bees are strong Hochstetler family traditions. My great-grandfather, and then Grandpa too, had beehives and orchards. Now my dad and most of my uncles on that side of the family have the same interests. Since Dad's retirement, he keeps himself busy with his fifty fruit trees, plus grapes, blueberries, blackberries, strawberries, and raspberries. Last but not least is his flourishing, weed-free vegetable garden.

Of course, much more could be written of the memories Dad talked about over the years, but I won't attempt to write everything. Dad put in a term of conscientious objector service during the war, and later came home and married my mother, Esther D. Hochstetler.

Life is easier now, in many ways, compared to those good old days. Dad is having his eighty-fourth birthday this summer, and my mom will have her eightieth on September 2. Dad, especially, has slowed down in recent years, and he is no longer able to do much gardening. But as my parents would say, "The important things, which have eternal value, are always the same." The psalmist puts it this way in Psalm 16:6 (KJV): "The lines are fallen unto me in pleasant places; yea, I have a goodly heritage."

Rhoda

~ *13* ~

Heaven Our Home

Sara Nolt

*M*y husband and I started dating while I was teaching school in a village in Ghana and he was more
than five thousand miles away in America. Aside from the
postal service, which delivered letters nearly a month after
they were sent, our communication was limited to email on
weekends and to phone calls once a month when I would
get to a city with reliable cell phone reception. *Reliable* is a
relative term, though, meaning my borrowed phone showed
enough bars of service to make a call without climbing a tree
to catch the signal, a trick that worked in the village. But the
city's cell phone coverage didn't mean connections were good.
Our conversations were plagued with phrases like "Are you
still there?" and "Can you hear me?" and "Sorry, I couldn't
catch that." Sometimes, dreadful silence told me we had lost
connection.

After months of sketchy communication, I flew back home,
knowing John would meet me at the airport. My small army
of pictures of him and the long-distance communication had

become poor substitutes for being together in person. John felt the same way.

"Anticipation is high on seeing you," he communicated with me. "If an earthly meeting can bring this much happiness and excitement, what will it be like when we get to heaven and can see Jesus?"

Being together in person was all we thought it would be. The pictures of John, which I dearly loved in our separation, weren't needed when we sat across a table, talking. I could watch his eyes twinkle when he laughed. I could hear his voice clearly now, with no miserable phone connection to cut our sentences short. Better than that, we could communicate with no words at all. Exchanging happy looks is a language of its own and totally possible when we were together.

John took me to my parents' home. The house I lived in since babyhood was filled with the same wonderful people, love, and happiness I remembered. Things I hadn't even realized I missed seemed to reach out to welcome me: soft, carpeted floors; couches long enough to stretch out on; a bookcase full of old friends; and even the familiar squeak of the front door. Home wrapped itself around me as a year's separation melted swiftly away. That separation had been the hardest thing of all. I missed out on holidays and special events. I missed family more than anything else in the world. It felt good to be surrounded by those I loved.

I look back on that homecoming and know that in it I have tasted a tiny fraction of the joys of heaven. The things that meant the most upon my return are only the dimmest shadows, the faintest whispers of heavenly things. And since these mere whispers bring so much satisfaction, my longing is deepened for the day when the joys of heaven are no longer shadowy whispers but thunders of reality.

One day we are going home. We are only soldiers on a tour of duty fraught with hardship, separation, and sometimes sketchy communication. But the day is coming when our assignment will be over, when we can lay down our sword and be surrounded with all the joys of home.

The end of separation. This is high on my list of things I look forward to in heaven. Being with Jesus in person will be far better than being with John, as much as I loved that reunion. I can hardly wait. Plus, although heaven isn't all about family reunions, we will eternally be together with those we are separated from now.

Ultimate connection. I want to talk with Jesus, to exchange wordless looks, to be able to communicate without the sketchy connection I sometimes feel I'm dealing with. Through the words of the Bible, I know he approves of me, but I look forward to hearing a physical voice tell me I've done well. I want to see his approval written on his face.

And I want to tell him in person that I'm so grateful for his suffering that made my entrance to heaven possible. I can't earn it. Even at my very best, I can't do a thing worthy of heaven. But his blood cloaks me in righteousness until I'm worthy of heaven.

Worship is one of those ways of communicating that I feel so limited here in this life. Between seeing heavenly things through a "glass darkly" and my own limitations, sometimes I feel that my worship is much too hindered. I want the real thing. In heaven, I will know what true worship is all about, and I look forward to an eternity of that.

The end of hard things. Life is full of hard things. Once, when my two sisters went back to the United States after three wonderful weeks of visiting me in Ghana, we cried together. When they left, a truly physical ache gripped my heart. As I closed the big metal gate behind them, my tears blurred the whole lonely world they left me in. It was hard.

I listened to a friend tell me about choices she is faced with, and about peer pressure, and about being laughed at by her friends for making wise decisions she'll never, ever regret. It is hard.

I read the news and hear about injustice, war, pain, and suffering. People are dying for their faith. And worse, people are dying without faith. It is unbelievably hard.

There are all kinds of hard. But in heaven, our home, we will be secure and safe, and suffering will end. Hard things will be done away with, and we will offer our battle wounds to Jesus, saying to him, "Jesus, it was hard. But on earth I believed that this moment would make up for all that pain. Your Word was right. If I could measure the suffering I went through on earth with this joy, it doesn't even come close to the glory you have enshrouded me in. You are worth it!"

Sometimes, or maybe often, hard things are a direct result of sin. Heaven will be an end of that too. No sin. No temptation. No Satan, with his deceptions and vices. I can hardly wait.

The culmination of missionary efforts. So you say you aren't "into" missions? Pardon me, but if you have a Christian heritage, you are probably grateful to the kind missionary who talked to your ancestors and caused them to believe in Christ. Because they did so, you know Jesus today and are invited to live in heaven tomorrow. There are still unbelievers, and there are still people telling them about Jesus.

Revelation 5:9 paints a picture of every tribe and language praising God around his throne, declaring his worth and praise and glory. It is the ultimate worship, the culmination of all Jesus did for the world. Every sermon preached, every counseling session given, every evening spent without a dad or husband because they were off doing kingdom work: all these will be more than rewarded in heaven.

Faith becomes sight. John told me he would pick me up at the airport. He said he was looking forward to being with me. Then faith in his words became reality when we were together. I saw love in his eyes, and though it surprised me that he would love me like that, it was indisputable, for three months later he married me.

It might be inconceivable, but we have only tasted a fraction of the love of Jesus. When we get to heaven, that faint shadow will be clear. While by faith we believe Jesus loved us enough to die for us, in heaven we will see it in his eyes. We will breathe it. Love that never fades or grows old will be eternal reality.

Today it can be hard to walk by faith in spiritual things. We like physical stuff. We like seeing where we are going and what we believe in. But much of Christianity requires great faith. In heaven the need for faith will be ended. There will be no more shame over realizing you lacked faith. Faith will become sight.

Are you still with me, reader? Heaven is your home. You were not meant to live forever where you are, faced with hard assignments, separations, sorrow, limited communication, and mere whispers of joy. You were created for something far greater than this.

You were created for the day you can lay down your sword and be done with hard things. You were created to be face-to-face with Jesus and to praise God throughout eternity. Your voice was born so it could join the throng at the foot of his throne. You were created for the day when whispers of heavenly things will be exchanged for the thundering praises sung by the ransomed around the world.

Very soon, homesick one, Jesus will come for us, and we will finally go home.

Sara

III Testimony

*W*hen we think of the word testimony, *we might think of a witness giving his statement in court, or of someone standing up before being baptized, declaring her salvation story. Writers are always witnesses. We watch other people and observe situations all around us, every scrap of story going into the compost pile for possible use later on. We watch our own lives even more closely.*

The following writers have been witnesses to their own stories, and here they tell them in the hopes we will gain more clarity and understanding of our own stories. Some of them involve traumatic, wounding circumstances, such as a stillborn baby and a child's seizure disorder. Other stories are far less heavy, although no less worthy of being told.

Sara Nolt reveals how her struggle with inferiority shaped her, first in negative ways and then in an emerging strength. "[In my perspective, my sister] was everything

I was not. Pretty. Talented. Creative. Effortlessly thin. Sang like an angel. Outgoing but not overbearing. Our worlds overlapped. . . . Ordinary me met above-average her everywhere I went."

I laughed out loud at the secondhand testimony of an Amish man whose wife accidentally bought extremely stretchy fabric to sew pants for him, and at Linda Byler's story about the time her son ate an entire head of lettuce.

Life is a mix of tragedy and triumph, grief and glee. Each of these stories is a testament to the power of telling our stories.

~ 14 ~

The Lord Is My Rock

ERVINA YODER

My labor began late in the evening of the first day of spring. Nine long months of pregnancy, many of which I spent bedridden with acute morning sickness, had finally turned into the countdown we'd been waiting for. I was one week overdue. My husband was so excited to be a daddy, and I was so excited to meet the cherished little person who had been forming inside my body for nearly a year. Our families were excitedly waiting by their phones for the announcement. After being awake all night with contractions, I was relieved when the sun finally rose on Friday, March 21. We put the finishing touches on our hospital bags, took a long walk, and headed for our midwife's office.

The contractions were five minutes apart when we found out our baby no longer had a heartbeat.

I gave birth one day, and the next I watched my husband shovel dirt onto a tiny grave. I went from the heights of expecting a perfectly healthy baby to the depths of shock and grief and the unimaginable pain of never seeing my firstborn son take a breath.

I cannot describe the sorrow. But I can describe the faithfulness of God in the midst of it. From the moment the ultrasound confirmed the silent heart and we heard the doctor's words—"Your baby is not alive"—a grace and peace were poured into my husband and me. These are unexplainable apart from Jesus Christ. We would need this supernatural strength in the days and weeks and months to come. The Scriptures I had meditated on, read aloud over my baby in my womb, and taped up in various places around my home to prepare for labor and delivery became alive and precious as never before. God had done so much in preparing my heart, removing my fears for childbirth, and strengthening me with his promises. Although the outcome turned out to be completely different than I ever dreamed, God's Word never lied, and his promises never failed.

In Psalm 16:8, David talks about setting the Lord always before him; he testifies, "Because he is at my right hand, I shall not be moved" (KJV). Thousands of years later, I'm learning the same thing holds true if I build my life around Jesus.

But other Scriptures are more challenging: "As for God, his way is perfect" (2 Samuel 22:31 KJV). Do I believe that—*truly* believe it—with a full-term pregnancy and a labor that turned into a mommy- and daddy-to-be's worst nightmare? No mistakes, no accidents, nothing outside God's control?

I don't believe the Lord took our son's life—that would be against God's very nature and character. But I do believe God allowed it to be taken for reasons not yet known (and which may never be fully known on this earth). I believe that he will work it for our good and for the honor of his name. I believe that, because this is who I know God to be. Because I couldn't survive such pain if I didn't. Because God's Word is consistent. Because God is the hope that anchors my soul. Because the way

before me is not unwalked; Jesus was a man of sorrows and acquainted with grief. If Jesus bore the weight of sin and endured
the cross so grace would triumph, and if God can turn the an-
guish of the cross into the place of love's greatest accomplish-
ment, how much more can he use any moment in our lives,
including this one, for his glory and the good of his people?

I think Charles Spurgeon sums it up beautifully: "Believing
that God rules all, that He governs wisely, that He brings good
out of evil, the believer's heart is assured, and he is enabled
calmly to meet each trial as it comes." God's sovereignty is the
greatest source of our peace; it's what sustains us, puts our un-
answered questions to rest, leans the weight of all our happiness
on him, and fills us with the hope of heaven.

* * *

Life for my husband and me has changed completely. What I
thought I'd be doing isn't happening. I miss my son terribly, and
reminders of our life without him are everywhere. The nursery
we spent hours preparing is empty. The adorable baby clothes I
bought at Goodwill and washed and folded never clothed our
child. Each tiny little diaper is still fresh and clean. We removed
the car seat from our back seat and gave the borrowed bassinet
back to our friends. I go grocery shopping and no one knows
I'm a mommy. Accepting such an enormous change is agoniz-
ingly difficult.

I have wondered what kind of purpose remains, if any. I re-
play the details of my pregnancy, my overdue labor, my delivery. I read the Psalms, over and over. I pray not to get lost in
my grief and for Jesus to guide me through it. "The greatest
good suffering can do for me," Joni Eareckson Tada said, "is
to increase my capacity for God." My desperate need for God
and my daily dependence on his grace to sustain me and be my

Rock has grown and deepened in incredible ways since we gave our baby back to God.

I never wanted to be a woman who understands heartbreak at such a deep level. I never wanted to give my child back so soon to the One who formed him within my body. I never wanted to be acquainted with this kind of intense sorrow. But there is no greater richness than to have life fall apart and still be unshaken because of a foundation of knowing who God is. To have no other hope but Jesus—to have only his truth and his promises sustain me—has given me an assurance of his presence that is precious beyond words.

In the agonizing grief of these last months, I have learned to lean all the weight of my soul on the Lord because he is the only solid rock I have. I have found him to be so near, so faithful, so sufficient, so redeeming.

I'm realizing just how much of a shadow life on this earth is compared to the glorious reality of eternity. I'm also realizing, slowly, that just because I have suffered great loss and just because I mourn so deeply does not mean life has been stripped of purpose. The truth is that Jesus is my life. And because he lives, for me to live is not motherhood; it's not being a wife; it's not being a woman known for ministry or hospitality, although all those things are good and honorable. For me to live is, simply, Christ. He is how I survive pain that should strip a person down to her natural response of anger, bitterness, and depression. Christ is whom I wake up for in the morning, how I make it through the day, and why I can rest peacefully at night.

Trials and pain are why this earth groans for the return of the Lord, and I groan with it. And the question for us as believers is, How do we live in pain, in loss, in heartbreak, in unbearable sorrow? How do we steady our hearts—not just survive—in a fallen world? How do we seek God's face, his purposes, and his joy so that he is glorified through our earthly bodies?

We search the Scriptures to know the character and person of God. We ask him to reveal himself in our lives. We build a foundation of truth instead of allowing emotions and circumstances to dictate and dominate our theology. We understand that everything the world offers as coping mechanisms and quick escapes from pain are only sinking sand. Instead, we stand on Christ, the solid Rock. We carry our burdens to him and allow our broken, humble lives to showcase to the world how good and faithful and trustworthy our God is.

Ervina

~ 15 ~

Overcoming Inferiority

SARA NOLT

I am ordinary. As we were growing up, one of my older sisters, Jenna, was everything I was not. Pretty. Talented. Creative. Effortlessly thin. Sang like an angel. Outgoing but not overbearing.

Our worlds overlapped. A lot. Ordinary me met above-average her everywhere I went. There is probably a group of people who still don't know I have a name. They know me as "Jenna's sister." One year we sang together in a community chorus. The next year I went by myself. The first person I met there said, "Hey! You are Jenna's sister, aren't you?" He looked beyond me hopefully. "Is she here?"

She wasn't. Disappointed, he walked on.

I was used to having people prefer Jenna, and in those days, it actually didn't bother me too much. I was shy and insecure. Jenna's outgoing personality was more of a crutch to me than a hang-up. I needed her confidence and her social strengths to carry me along. She drove whenever we went anywhere. She talked to the cashiers. She had the friends and the social life.

I was just happy to be her friend and thankful she didn't mind having me with her.

But one day Jenna got married and moved seventeen hours away. This was so much more than a wonderful sister marrying Prince Charming at a beautiful wedding. This was the day I lost my best friend, social life, and identity—all with a simple "I do."

After the wedding, I wrote to one of Jenna's friends, who had been kind to me, and said, "The Bible says all things work together for good, but I can see no good thing in this for me!"

Not only did Jenna move away, but I, the socially inept one, had to take her job as secretary for my dad's business. That meant I had to answer the phone and interact with real people, which was terrifying, at least at first. But God showed me that my shyness wasn't honoring him. I wanted God to be able to use me in his kingdom, but I was sadly hindered by my shyness.

The office job helped to strip that shyness away. The office also gave me spare time that I used on book studies, memorizing Scripture, and reading missionary biographies. These things nurtured my ever-growing desire to be used in God's kingdom. I took several mission trips in those days, including a yearlong teaching position in Africa.

Those years were growing ones. The shyness, the insecurities, the underlying sense of inferiority seemed to be melting away. I was growing my own social wings and gaining an identity of my own.

Then—oh, wonder of wonders!—I got married. My husband is amazing.

He also happens to be Jenna's brother-in-law.

* * *

My new husband and I ended up moving to the area where Jenna and her husband lived, and we began attending their church. Suddenly all those old feelings and insecurities resurfaced. Jenna already had a place carved out for herself within the church. Jenna was in our small Wednesday evening group that met in homes. Jenna was at every family reunion I attend—now on both sides.

My old insecurities hit me full force. I knew how to be Jenna's sister as a shy teen, but I didn't know how to relate to her now that I had wings of my own. In groups, I naturally reverted to being the old, quiet me when she was there. It felt right to let her have the friends, talk to the people, and lead out.

But something was rebelling within me. *This wasn't who I was.* I had an identity. Or did I?

Suddenly I started looking at Jenna in a different way. I began comparing myself to her and decided that even in my prime, I came up short. This beautiful, talented sister of mine outshone me in everything. Again. I felt insignificant.

The hollow aloneness gave way to periods of discouragement. Often there wasn't any specific incident to be discouraged about; it was just a heavy load of feeling insignificant and inferior. The feelings ran deep. I could see no way out. How does a two-talented person or even a seven-talented person constantly rub shoulders with ten-talented people and not come away feeling inferior? Was it even possible?

Inferiority, that ruthless taskmaster, ruled me well. Things that should have been insignificant became points of discouragement. One of my trigger points was spending time with somebody accomplished. In fact, by this time, I could feel inferior around many different people, for Jenna was no longer my only object of comparison. Others' accomplishments made me feel of little worth, and an overwhelming loneliness wrapped itself around my heart. I had periods of listlessness and disinterest in everything.

My husband, a perpetual optimist, would suggest, "Let's pray about it." I knew he was right, but many times I could form no prayers of my own. Undeterred, he would pray. Having his prayers wash over me renewed my faith and helped me rise out of the darkness once again.

I also spoke to a couple of friends about my issue. Their responses were basically the same thing: "What? You feel this way? I would never have guessed! And, honestly . . ." and then they'd tell me where I excelled. They'd talk about my strong points and my talents. I'd walk away feeling better, but the comfort was hollow and empty and didn't last. Now I understand that their well-intended words only aided me in the comparison game—assistance I didn't need. I was a pro in comparing myself to others. And I was beginning to hate who I was.

It was my mother-in-law who offered my first glimmer of hope. After I sobbed out my story to her, she simply nodded and said, "The ground is level at the foot of the cross."

Immediately, I pictured the cross of Jesus with a multitude kneeling before it. I was there with my superiors—only, they weren't superior anymore. All pedestals and titles were cast away. The cross brought equality.

"The blood is our only hope of eternal life," my mother-in-law continued. "All the other things you mentioned are the peripherals of life. Being talented or having a great personality might add beauty to life, but when it comes to what matters in eternity, we are all equals."

Hope wove its way into my heart. For the first time in my life, I caught sight of life beyond inferiority. In the coming weeks, whenever I was tempted to feel insignificant, I immediately put myself at the foot of the cross and sang its victory song: "It doesn't matter if she is excelling, for the ground is level at the foot of the cross!"

I was amazed at the freedom this truth brought, and I walked in its glory for months. And then that old devil, unwilling to let his longtime slave go free, repositioned himself and attacked the old wound from a fresh angle.

* * *

This time my struggle had to do with spiritual things. I saw people being used in God's kingdom and I felt left behind. Making a difference in lives of people mattered to me. All my old feelings came flooding back, to the point that I wondered if even Jesus saw me as subpar.

I wanted inner change. Surely God had something better for his children! So I fasted and prayed, and mercifully, God answered. He answered by revealing the root causes of my problem.

It came through a sermon our pastor preached. "Everybody loves themselves," the preacher said in that pivotal message. I suppressed a snort. Didn't he know that I, a regular attender, hated myself completely?

"You *do* love yourself," he continued, as if he could read my thoughts. "You might not like when self isn't the hero you want it to be, but you do love yourself. The Bible says no man has ever hated his own flesh."

In that moment, I knew he was right. I finally recognized the connection between pride and the sadness that overwhelmed me when I felt insignificant.

For all these years, I thought I knew what I was dealing with. I thought I hated myself and had a low self-esteem. But God's diagnosis was different. He revealed my heart to be full of jealousy, envy, pride, and a love of self. Indeed, pride has two faces. One is easily recognized by its haughty superiority; the other is disguised behind a mask of low self-esteem. I had always thought that self-hatred was the opposite of pride. How could a shy, inferior-feeling one be proud? And then I saw it: I loved myself as any proud person does. I wanted myself to be loved and recognized by others.

About the time I listened to that revealing message, a sister at church loaned me a book that described jealousy and envy. I sat there, stunned. It was describing me.

My immediate response to these awful diagnoses—pride and jealousy—was relief. If you are ill and have no idea what is wrong, you can't run for the cure. But hope of a transformation was born in me when I finally understood the roots of my chronic discouragement and the heaviness of inferiority.

By God's grace, transformation finally happened to me. Just understanding my root issues helped me shun feelings I once gave in to. Change didn't happen effortlessly. But the following is a list of ways that help me walk in continual victory. I pray that these will do the same for you should you ever be tempted to feel inferior.

Guard your thoughts. The battle of inferiority is won or lost in our minds. And a hard battle it is! Years of wrong thought processes are not easily corrected, but victory is dependent on our thought life. "As he thinketh in his heart, so is he," says Proverbs 23:7 (KJV). Dwelling on our own perceived failures, dumb things we have said or done, and how we do not match up to people around us creates the hollow sadness associated with feeling inferior.

Take God's Word seriously when it says to bring "into captivity every thought" (2 Corinthians 10:5 KJV). Measure your thoughts against Philippians 4:8: "Whatsoever things are true, whatsoever things are honest, whatsoever things are just, whatsoever things are pure, whatsoever things are lovely, whatsoever things are of good report; if there be any virtue, and if there be any praise, think on these things" (KJV). If your thoughts do not pass each category listed here, reject them and replace them with God-honoring thoughts.

Thinking on things that are true means not living in a fantasy world. In fantasy worlds, the dreamer is always the heroine, the one with the intelligent response, and the winner of every debate. But then the dreamer has to return to a real world. Fantasy worlds are no place for you. Live in the moment, trusting God with your weaknesses and holding on to his victory for tomorrow.

Do not compare yourself with others. This is a killer. Comparing ourselves causes us to feel either superior or inferior to someone else. Neither outcome is God-honoring.

Know your position in Christ. Meditate on verses that speak of God's love and acceptance. The Bible says that we are "accepted in the beloved" (Ephesians 1:6 KJV). Let your confidence in who you are be based on God's approval of you. He sees the blood that covers you and declares you fit for life with him, regardless of how you are feeling about yourself. You are God's child, an heir of a King. Let your life reflect that.

Learn to accept compliments, and never degrade yourself. Don't deflect kind words that come to you. Compliments are a rare part of life and were meant to make the moment a positive one. Let it be just that. Hand in hand with that is to never degrade yourself. You are a divinely designed masterpiece. Don't discredit the Potter who created you by telling him what a terrible design you are.

Find a friend who will pray for you. You do not need people to shore up the sinking foundation of your self-esteem with kind but hollow praise. You need people who will reaffirm your position in Christ and pray for your victory. On many dark days, when I hadn't the emotional stamina to form prayers of my own, listening to my husband pray for me rebuilt my faith and lifted me out of the depression I was in.

Do something else. Sitting alone in my quiet house with dark thoughts was an excellent way to slide into discouragement. Taking a walk, getting some groceries, going outside, or even calling someone on the phone helped to shake the thoughts before they ruined my day. Do something for someone else if you have nothing pressing at home.

Use the Bible as your sword. I have a Bible-verse-a-day app on my phone. Whenever I'm tempted to feel blue about who I am, I tap that verse and meditate on it. It has been helpful in warding off the temptation to be discouraged. But you don't need an app. You can memorize verses or write them on cards the old-fashioned way, posting them where you can see them.

Pray for love. Perfect love for God casts out fear that we are not good enough. Perfect love for others lets us love them and rejoice with them even when their gifts overshadow our own.

I experienced immediate victory when I first understood the roots of my defeat. But it wasn't until after a few months of consciously conditioning my mind with new thought patterns that I recognized my change.

I had just ended a conversation with my mother-in-law, Joan, when the phone rang. It was Joan, calling with a clarification. "I just wanted to make sure you knew I wasn't comparing your talents to Jenna's . . ." It was a joyful moment to realize that I had not even been tempted to take her words that way.

It was like having a wound on your finger finally heal. When it is sore, you notice your finger in everything you do. But when the wound has healed, you can go days before you consciously think about your fingers at all. My sensitivity to the debilitating feelings of inferiority was being healed.

Inner change, that coveted transformation, had finally come.

Sara

Seized by Grace

STEPHANIE J. LEINBACH

$\mathcal{S}$he thrust her fist into her cereal bowl and shattered our
world.

Until that moment, we were an ordinary family living an ordinary life. But on that ordinary Saturday morning, Tarica said,
"Mom, sometimes I can't move my arm." As if it were a signal,
her fist splashed into her milk, her head tipped sideways, and
she stared sightlessly through me.

With that seizure, we left ordinary behind.

Medical dramas always happen to someone else, not me.
I remember the disbelief a few days later, the feeling of being
apart from my own body, watching as a seizure robbed our
daughter of her very breath. I remember my husband's violent
prayer of denial over her blue and convulsing body. I remember
I couldn't remember how to dial 911.

At Children's Hospital of Pittsburgh, doctors ordered tests
and pumped Tarica full of anti-seizure drugs. She stopped seizing and started screaming. For twelve nonstop hours, Tarica
fought Linford and me like a rabid animal, recoiled from the

monsters she saw on the walls, laughed and held out her hands to baby Jesus, and looked at me and asked, "Who are you?" I could almost hear my heart break over the screaming, screaming, screaming.

Sometime during the night, Linford said, "If this is what she's going to be like, I would rather she . . ."

He didn't finish. Although I understood his feelings, that night forged the iron in my soul. Seizures would not devour us. This medical drama was a short detour, a brief deviation from normal, but we would find ordinary again. Soon.

In the morning, the doctors put Tarica on less hallucinatory drugs. The tests eventually gave Tarica a diagnosis: epilepsy. We ended our four-day stay with a bulging folder of paperwork, two anti-epilepsy drug prescriptions, and several upcoming doctor appointments. But we didn't take home Tarica; we took home a wildcat.

Tarica had always gotten along well with her older sister, Jenica. But now our drugged wildcat fought and snarled and showed her claws constantly. I spent my days watching for seizures and settling fights, struggling to discipline a child transformed by drugs.

Shock fogged my brain. My prayers were reduced to the tears I wiped onto my infant Micah's fuzzy head and three words— "Help me, God."

* * *

From shock grew determination. I went on a research binge, looking for options, anything but drugs. I found none that would work for Tarica's specific situation and seizure type.

By now, the seizures had subsided, the monster in her head drugged into submission. But the side effects of the drugs— irritability, anger, extreme drowsiness, and continual stomachaches—stunted her life.

Four months after diagnosis, the seizures returned. First one seizure, then another, until they came once a day, twice a day, accelerating. We increased her medication to the maximum dose. Three seizures a day. Two medications became three. Four, five, six, seven seizures a day, plus who knows how many at night. Another dose adjustment, one drug added, another weaned. She seized and seized, uncontrolled.

Four months of seizures lurched by. A week before her fifth birthday, Tarica had a new kind of seizure. It knocked her over, lasted twice as long, and temporarily paralyzed her left side. That morning at an appointment in Pittsburgh, we discussed brain surgery. We had a decision to make.

The new seizures became normal. She collapsed every time she seized. No more stairs or standing on chairs, unless she had someone beside her.

The violent seizures should have upset me, but I saw in them a sign. Something had to be done to give Tarica her life back. We had been asking God what to do. Brain surgery looked like her best option.

Tarica was admitted for phase 1 of the surgery process. This involved extensive testing to see if tests could locate the seizure focus (source) within her brain. If the tests found the focus, then she would qualify for phase 2: brain surgery. Phase 1 usually took ten days to record all the necessary seizures. Because Tarica had so many seizures, her tests took six days, the shortest phase 1 in the hospital's records. The tests quickly found the seizure focus.

After phase 1, Tarica stopped seizing, but we scheduled phase 2. With Tarica's history, the doctors didn't believe she'd remain seizure-free. Besides, a young, resilient brain responds better to surgery.

I could see where our story was going. God was showering his grace on us and revealing his power. Surgery would heal

Tarica, and we'd have a miraculous story to tell. No more drugs. The real Tarica would return.

Oh, I rejoiced to see God at work. Some of the work had happened in my own heart. Our epilepsy detour taught me that I don't get to map my journey—or my daughter's. Epilepsy was a detour only because I had other plans—ones not involving drugs, hospitals, and seizures. I wanted the gentle road winding through the shady foothills, not this pockmarked path plunging through thorns and staggering beside black canyons that threatened to swallow me.

I learned I don't appreciate God's grace until it's all I have left—and then I reach out, desperate, and grace seizes me. By grace, I am borne through the darkest nights and hardest questions. Like manna, grace cannot be hoarded. There's always enough to sustain me, but never so much that I forget to depend on God. Grace made me feel as helpless as epilepsy did, because I couldn't control it. Epilepsy seized Tarica. Grace seized me.

I learned that I made epilepsy harder by believing that God didn't intend this path for us. Not for a lifetime, certainly. He had given us a detour long enough to teach us a few lessons, and then he'd guide us back to the gentle road.

I learned that when I try to plan a detour's route, I end up lost. And lost is where I found myself in the next part of our story.

* * *

Tarica was weaned off her medication and admitted for phase 2. The surgeon implanted a temporary grid in her brain over the seizure focus. She had to seize at least twice while the grid was in so the doctors could zero in on the precise location of the focus. After that, if all went well, the surgeon would remove the seizure focus.

We waited ten days. No seizures. All kinds of abnormal brain activity, typical of epilepsy, yes, plenty of that, but not one seizure. The doctors were baffled. Was this the same girl who had a six-day phase 1?

On day ten, Tarica was wheeled to the operating room for the grid removal surgery. I stood beside her as she slid onto the operating table and accepted the anesthesia mask. When the drugs overpowered her, I released her hand and stepped back. A nurse led me out of the room, and as the doors swung shut behind us, I bent at the waist as if I had been kicked in the stomach, and I wept into my hands.

The nurse laid her hand on my shoulder. "She'll be okay. She's in good hands."

"No, no, it's not that," I choked. "It's that we went through all this for nothing."

In the last ten days, I had learned brutal lessons about faith and trust and grace, but at what cost? Tarica wasn't healed.

We took her home, brain intact, back on medication. We feared she'd seize soon after surgery, but she's been seizure-free for over two years.

Does this mean she's healed—not by surgeon's blade but by God's power? I don't know. Her latest EEG revealed the same abnormal brain activity that's been present since her first EEG. The doctors say she could seize at any moment. They don't offer much hope, outside of a miracle, that she'll live her life without seizures. But right now she's not seizing.

There aren't words enough to express our gratefulness to God. She is in second grade and doing very well with her schoolwork. Thank God her brain survived all the trauma. She's still on medication and probably will be all her life. The next hurdle is getting through puberty. Hormonal changes very often trigger seizures in girls with epilepsy.

For now, the monster in her brain sleeps, and we pray it will never wake. But if it does, God's grace will arm us to rise and meet it with courage.

I'm done trying to map our route. Because epilepsy taught me a lesson I'll never forget. No matter what road conditions lie ahead, the God who led me through the thorns, who fished me out of a few canyons, who seized me with his grace—that same God will be there.

He will be there beside us on the road that isn't a detour after all.

Stephanie

~ *17* ~

Season of Doubt

SHEILA PETRE

One Monday near the end of January, I wrote these things to do in my planner: Cut out lavender dress. Make pie crusts. Write circle letter. Study the Trinity. Do laundry. Supper: cheeseburger soup and breadsticks.

All morning, I churned through the laundry, and it was a mountain. By lunchtime, supper's hamburger was thawing and the cheeseburger soup base was prepared. But I had not even begun to fold the wash. The lavender fabric was still a heap on the sewing cabinet, and I had postponed the pie crusts.

One thing had taken priority: I had begun to study the Trinity, and I found these amazing words of Jesus: "All power is given unto me in heaven and in earth. Go ye therefore, and teach all nations, baptizing them in the name of the Father, and of the Son, and of the Holy Ghost: Teaching them to observe all things whatsoever I have commanded you: and, lo, I am with you always, even unto the end of the world" (Matthew 28:18-20 KJV).

Why were these words amazing? Because that school year we were hosting Nikki, a Muslim exchange student from

Azerbaijan, and she had been challenging me, often, that I worship three gods, not one. "Did God make Jesus?" she asked. And how can God be born of a woman when the Qur'an says the world is under the foot of a woman, and any son of a woman must acknowledge her superiority, and how could Mary be superior to God?

My conversations with Nikki prompted a series of questions. What *is* my religion founded on? How do our religions differ? I was interested. In the spirit of research, I borrowed a book from the library that neutrally discussed religious history. (Or not so neutrally. The writer, a theology teacher, was a former Christian.)

Perhaps it was this book; perhaps it was a mind pried open by stress; I am sure it was a native fault line in my spirit. Doubt shoved a foot in my door. So maybe Islam isn't a true religion. But is Christianity?

The Bible: Is it true?

Trust is a bridge stretching from the speaker to the listener, from the writer to the reader. On a gray day in February, I listened to one of my favorite speakers discuss the hope of consolation. He quoted Jesus' words: "I am with you always" (Matthew 28:20). That was the day I realized, with dismay, how strong my doubt had grown. I watched its chisel chip away splinters of that bridge until it was so narrow I could not trust it to carry me to comfort.

So Jesus said it? I thought, and my thought had the metallic tang of sarcasm. So who is he? What difference does he make in my life?

Mother Teresa, I am told, doubted most of her life through, but served anyway. Was her mind the only thing Satan could subjugate? I wondered. Or was her doubt a reasonable one: a superior intellect glimpsing the certainty of a godless universe?

One day I stood at my back door, watching the children play in the snow, and contemplated Mother Teresa—and myself. I felt adrift. Alone. Where can one turn for assurance when the place one has turned to in the past is a book riddled with inconsistencies?

I turned to it anyway. I found something: in the Bible, doubt is invariably followed by rebuke. I cower from rebuke. In the kitchen, in conversation, or in my writing tablet, I am quick and confident, tossing words or salads as though I think myself a master. But tap me with a reprimand, especially one regarding my character or spirituality, and I am all snail, my witty indifference a shell elaborately coiled. How much worse when God is the one reprimanding. Or—how much better.

When someone rebukes me, he or she does so after examining one shard of my person. The God of the Bible knows all, sees all, and rebukes doubt, which is sin.

Be merciful, O God, my God. If in your perfection, your divinity, you are three persons, convince me. Does the Holy Spirit remain in the heart where the chosen Son is doubted? I trust so; I must. Very early on, the godly line paused almost a century, and Abraham and Sarah, the couple standing at the gap, doubted it would begin again. Yet it did.

* * *

For long months, I paused also. I doubted. Doubt clouded the words I spoke and the words I wrote. Doubt shadowed me when I read Bible stories to my children—more of them than usual, for I could not let my sin taint my children. Doubt shadowed my future.

I prayed, vaguely, for wisdom. I prayed, specifically, for belief.

At last I crept back.

I did not throw myself on God's mercy any more than I have ever cuddled in his arms. But I opened myself to it, cautiously. For I knew that if God is, there is no one's anger I fear more and no one's approval I as desperately crave. For God to be God—both merciful and angry—he must have parts of himself that I cannot understand. For me, a human, to decide that such parts disprove him is a gross sin of willful ignorance.

"I had a time of intense doubt right after my conversion," my friend Annette told me. "What brought me back was the creation. The indisputable creation."

It was that which finally beckoned me back to safety. This world is too intricate, too articulate, to be fashioned by anything but a Mystery. A perfect being, singular. A God. The God. Dare I say my God?

And if he is God, then, could not One who knits together bones in the womb and plans an oriole's nest and designs the mystery of marriage speak through a Spirit—the same message into many vessels? Could God not speak to these men who wrote the words that could bring peace millennia later?

Such a God would not talk to one person in an exclusive language. He wouldn't hide behind visions or send his messengers warring across a landscape, spewing blood into an insecure future.

As a poet, I thrive on analogy, and though you may say that my upbringing has skewed my reality, I see analogies everywhere. Dawn assures me of heaven. Loneliness whines of hell. A blade of wheat proves the resurrection. One who plans the geometry of a spider's web, the bursting of a wineberry's casing, and the castle rooms of a columbine could plan vaster things. He could understand the trappings of sin, provide an escape, and finally prepare a place for us.

In the eyes of many witnesses, Jesus died. The enemy himself saw Jesus buried, and he snickered for two brief days. But Jesus rose, appearing again before many witnesses. These things are recorded for me, and no conniving mortal mind could spin such a mystery.

What I can see proves God, and what I can't see proves his plan of salvation. If I believe in God, will I not believe what he says? Then God is three.

Yet is he, triune God, honored when I return to him by a winding way of reason? Ah, but I also prayed in faith, begging for wisdom and belief.

In one of my favorite poems, Janice Etter writes about unbelief: "Lives lie bleakly frozen, in want of fire or salt." She adds, "Belief, like love, is chosen, and never by default."

Closing my eyes to my native doubt, I backed into belief: as winter wore into spring and all the earth echoed resurrection, nature defied the nonexistence of God.

I turned to face a personal God. Too long he had been obscured behind the veil flung across my eyes by one who sought not a relationship but revenge.

Through that bleak winter, as I wrestled with my doubt, my faith a shriveled mustard seed watered by tears, I wondered. Perhaps the only difference between belief and unbelief is whether or not we are still thinking. To be an atheist, I would have to stop thinking. I would have to close a door in my mind and pretend a room, vaster than myself, does not exist.

When it came down to this, I knew what to choose. By the grace of God, and with the aid of the Holy Spirit, purchased by the power of Jesus' perfect blood willingly shed, I choose to keep thinking. The mustard seed has sprouted. I can't see it . . . I can't feel it . . . but God is merciful.

God is. He is with me, even to the end of the world.

Sheila

18

Stretched

Mary Troyer

I knew a lady who once bought some stretchy pants material for her husband and sewed him a pair. She just didn't know how stretchy the fabric actually was.

Her husband tried on the pants one evening, and they fit fine. They were hung by the suspenders on a hook overnight.

The next morning he put them on, and they seemed a little longer than they had the night before. He went on his way to work at five thirty in the morning. As the day wore on, he thought these new pants felt strange. But he had lots of work to get done, so he got busy, and only in the forenoon did he go to the bathroom to look at himself.

He was horrified at how he looked, and he wondered why his wife didn't tell him how awful those pants fit him! He didn't know what else to do but plunge ahead with his job, but in a very humbled way!

As the day continued, the new pants became bigger and longer. By one o'clock, he thought probably 1,500 people had seen him in those awful-looking pants. He was very relieved when two o'clock came so he could start for home.

He wanted to get on his bike, but by then he could not get his leg over the bar on the first try. So he had to pull up his pant leg to get his foot across. He reached into his pocket to get the house key, and his pocket was way down by his knee. By that time he was walking on his pant legs, as the suspenders and pants had stretched so much.

While on his way home, he thought about the traffic that was coming from behind him and seeing how he was dressed, with everything so stretched and big. The people would think he was dressed in modern style, the pants were so low.

Needless to say, he was happy when he finally got home so he could change into decent outerwear.

I'm sure his wife got a lecture on shopping for proper pants material. Knowing her, she had a good laugh.

Mary

19

The Horse That Wouldn't Budge

MARIE COBLENTZ

*F*all is upon us, maybe even winter. Oh, how I used to love winter! Sledding was a favorite of mine. I remember one time my brother and I went sledding. We were lying on a sled, whooshing down the pasture hill, when we struck a frozen manure pile and I hit it with my head. I had a good egg-sized bump and a black-and-blue eye for a while.

Many people approach old age with dread and misgivings because they haven't prepared for it. Youth look forward to a happy, useful life, but they rarely look ahead into old age. When we are young, we would do well to learn some creative skills that take little physical ability, in preparation for the time when we will naturally slow down.

Older people can also learn to do new things, of course. Lack of self-confidence, rather than lack of ability, is usually what causes older people to hesitate to try new projects. Life can be full in every age. Abraham was seventy-five years old when the

Lord led him into a strange country. Moses was all of eighty years when he was called to lead the people of Israel out of bondage.

I need to share a happening with you that hubby and I encountered in these vast Ohio hills. At the time it did not seem so funny, but all's well that ends well.

Recently on a Sunday morning, we headed south to church. We figured it would take us a good hour and a half, so we planned to start early. Besides, we had a borrowed horse that day, as ours was a little sick. We studied the map well and had our route planned just right.

Well, maps are not always so great. We go down this road and want to turn right onto the second road, and then we'll be almost there. We drive quite a ways and see the first road. And now the second one should be almost here, we think, when we come to another road, but the sign does not match the one on our map. We turn right anyway. The hill is steep and the road is soft and has huge gravel stones.

A little way up the hill, the horse decides no more of this, and he will not budge. I don't know whether to cry or not. Hubby says he has no idea where we are and that it's time to be there. These ministers try to be in good time.

We turn around, which the horse gladly does, probably hoping to go home. At the bottom of the hill, we stop and ask directions. Quite a distance back, we saw this path go into a field close to where we thought our road should be. Well, this is a private path that leads to our road.

So we turn around and start up this path when *again* our horse decides, no more hills. Now what? We know we're on the right track, and it's the second place across the field. But how far is it? And it's high time to be there.

There is a farm at the bottom of the hill, so this granny walks down to see if anyone is home. I'm sure this would've been quite a sight to see. A frustrated grandma with bonnet and shawl flopping, knocking on a stranger's door on a Sunday morning.

Oh yes, a kind old lady answers the door and says it's the second place over, and if you have good legs, you can walk. And yes, you may put your horse in our barn.

Well, I go back to hubby, and you guessed it: the horse decides to go if hubby leads him. So Granny comes huffing and puffing from behind. Finally we're on the right track. We let this borrowed horse walk until we get there. After all, he has put on some extra miles.

We arrive just in the nick of time and yes, we are welcome. All's well that ends well. We thank God for a good day! Such is life in these Holmes County hills.

Marie

Bone Opp-a-Deet!

LINDA BYLER

Through the summer months, nothing drains my reserve of happiness and goodwill faster than thinking about cooking supper. Seriously, what is an overheated, overweight, disgruntled housewife—having gone through life without a smidgen of talent pertaining to all things culinary—supposed to do? It's tough. A sad world.

Furthermore, this plight is enhanced by having entered holy matrimony with a man who has an extreme sense of taste and smell and by having the youngest offspring carry the same gene. That combination—lack of culinary skill and two picky eaters—has caused me great and debilitating anxiety. In plain words: I hate to cook.

First of all (and this is the truth), I do make weak attempts at becoming a better cook. This takes the form of flopping on the recliner, flapping my arms, hiking up my skirt, and taking a cookbook in hand. Yesterday it was Lena Yoder's cookbook. I had all good intentions of finding an interesting dish to go with the package of tilapia I had on hand. Fish is good. Fish is always good.

Anyway, I paged through the book with an ever-growing sense of having lost my way, as if I were reading an algebra book from high school. Dinner rolls, haystack meals, casseroles: all of it was clean over my head. Missing ingredients. Too much bother. I had only one hour.

Finally, I sighed with defeat and put the cookbook away. I made potatoes cut in small squares, boiled in salted water, drained, fried in olive oil, and sprinkled with seasoned salt. I made a small dish of coleslaw, and fried the fish with cracker crumbs, eggs, and more olive oil.

Our son Chris came home from work, threw his lunch and thermos on the counter, and said he had to go, don't keep supper. My husband, Gid, ate the fish. No coleslaw, no potatoes. Why? Why? If he brings home a bucket of Kentucky Fried Chicken, he loves their coleslaw and always comments on it. Well, let it be known: I will not try to find out how they make it. If it is so much better than mine, then so be it.

Lunches are much the same. Gid eats no sandwiches, no cereal, no potato chips, only certain kinds of bologna and cheese cut in squares . . . the list goes on and on. Gid and Chris always remember to tell me what was wrong with their lunch in order to acquire a more decent array of victuals for the following day. The other day Chris complained about having nothing green in his lunch. So the next day I put in a whole head of lettuce. He likes raw vegetables—broccoli, cauliflower, celery, and so on—and my groceries were low. So his lunch the day before had been high in carbohydrates in the form of stale cookies, moldy bread, and limp potato chips. You know how it goes when you're trying to make the groceries last awhile.

The head of lettuce was really funny, though, I admit. Chris said the guy he was working for laughed and laughed. It was a whole head of romaine lettuce, and Chris ate the whole thing.

* * *

I have taken desperate measures in the past too. One time, after a detailed complaint from the good husband, I refused to pack his lunch. I sent an empty lunchbox, with an ice pack and instructions to purchase his own food at the local coffee shop.

He eyed his wife in disbelief, but the housewife stood her ground. So he went off to work and did just that—bought himself packages of snacks and bags of bologna and cheese at the store. This went on for a few weeks. Gid was a good sport about it. He knew he had overstepped his bounds. So he'd sort of grin cheesily and go off to work.

Eventually, though, my conscience turned from a minor annoyance to flaming hot discomfort. I was afraid I was not coming under the label of a virtuous woman, or a submissive one, and I was certainly not even close to being sweet and loving, as behooves the feminine vessel.

There were no bad feelings for either of us, I don't believe, heh heh! (As you can tell, I'm trying to make us look better on paper than we really are.) But the truth is, cooking supper and packing lunches remain the least favorite parts of my day. They are necessary chores and that is absolutely it.

I doubt that any major change is on the horizon, either. I just turned sixty, so why start now when soon the golden era of stewed soda crackers and bean soup is all that our toothless gums will be able to handle? Taste buds deteriorated, we'll be happily slopping up peas in milk and soft-boiled eggs with week-old bread. I think that will be so delightful, eating that old Doddy and Mommy stuff, setting it out in the pan it was cooked in and opening a can of red beets and a jar of applesauce.

Then, of course, it's doubly humbling to have daughters who love to cook and who have come up with their own versions of soups and stews and canned pickles and relishes and who make their own bread and all that virtuous, outrageous stuff.

My daughter Becky says she chunks all her extra zucchini into small squares, places them in a plastic bag, and throws them in the freezer. That is what gives her vegetable soup its delicious flavor. Now how would you discover that? Knowing my fate, I'd make homemade vegetable soup and the men would ask what the green stuff is and bend over the bowl with a microscope. But ever eager to change my ways, I, too, chunked my zucchini and froze it this year. The end results will be posted at a later date.

And so forth. *Sigh.*

Daughter Laura gets a magazine called *Bon Appétit* (Bone Opp-a-Deet). I learned the pronunciation from her too. She told me the other day she made a fruit tart with a special crust made with butter, rolled out like pie dough, and then chilled in the refrigerator. Then she rolled blueberries in cornstarch and put them in the center of the dough, brought up the corners until . . .

Well, I don't know what she said after that, because my eyes started spinning in circles and glazed over and I entered my dead zone where my ears stop hearing. She thinks I might make something involving chilled dough? And how in the world would you roll blueberries in cornstarch? And then put them in the middle of a round of chilled dough? If I did that I'm pretty sure most of that dough would end up on the floor. And the blueberries would end up under the refrigerator or the stove, with me in a dubious position with a yardstick, fishing said blueberries out from under gas appliances.

At least I'm smart enough to know my limits.

Linda

IV WONDER

This short-but-sweet section easily could have been filed under "Testimony," as all four pieces are testimonies, but they are stories of a particular kind. They are true stories of miracles, phenomenal happenings that don't make sense from a human perspective. There's the account of a mother who sees her little one standing in the middle of a busy highway in front of their farm, knowing she will be too late to save her little girl. What happens next is a marvel.

Witness "God's Protecting Hand," the story of how God protected a peaceful Amish family from great harm during a home invasion. I have read accounts of thieves taking advantage of the Amish and Mennonite stand on nonresistance. The bad guys know that they won't face violent retribution, so these peace-loving folk are easy targets. Yet though this family was totally vulnerable from an earthly perspective, heaven's angels held them all in safekeeping. The verse that came to my mind is from Zechariah: "Not by might, nor by power, but by my Spirit, says the LORD of hosts" (Zechariah 4:6 ESV).

Danielle Beiler tells how she began to think of all her money coming from "God's bank account." Her story of God's wondrous—even miraculous—provision lingered in my mind and encouraged me many times after reading it. And Sherry Gore's remarkable story about a tough Thanksgiving and a car named Zippy? You can hardly read a paragraph without tripping over the miracles.

Yes, these stories could have been filed under "Testimony," but I wanted to highlight the awe-inspiring power of miracles. Let's keep our eyes and ears open to the possibility of supernatural intervention. Let's open our hearts to wonder.

Lorilee

~ 21 ~

The Angels' Charge

CATHERINE GASCHO

*I*t was an awesome spring day. Everything smelled wonderful, and it was a good feeling to be alive. The children were playing outdoors, and I was doing laundry.

Stepping out the door, I noticed three-year-old Emily and fourteen-month-old Lori playing at the water hydrant. Not wanting them to be soaking wet, I took them to the front of the garage on the cement to bike with Benjamin, age four. They were playing, so I reentered the house and started down the stairs.

Then I heard Benjamin scream. I knew we had a problem. My mind went immediately to Lori, who was fascinated by the road in front of our house. A couple from our church lives directly across the road, which only increased the temptation for her to toddle across for a visit.

As I rushed through the door, Lori started across the road. The other two were screaming. Running down the driveway, I couldn't see anything coming from either direction. Lori turned around and looked back as she heard us. By then, however, cars were coming and I kept running, hoping I could flag them down and make them stop.

Toddling back across the road, she held her hands up to me with a smile on her face. Then I saw it . . . the approaching car, headed toward her. There was no way to stop the car. It was going much too fast.

My knees almost crumpling, I ran on while my mind screamed, "Lori, this is your end!"

I was about three feet from the road when *whooosh!* The car barreled between us. I shook all over and almost fell down. There she was, standing in the center of the road. Shaking all over, I picked her up and carried her back to the house.

A little while later a friend called and asked if Lori had been out on the road. A customer at their shop had arrived, shaking. "Nothing matters," the customer had said. "We almost saw a child get killed! The car swerved and missed her."

That evening, my husband bought cattle panels, and we made a small enclosed play area for Lori. As he was putting them together, she tried climbing over. But they worked! I was so thankful to be a bit more relaxed when she was outside. Only two weeks earlier, her father Stephen had found her when she had climbed a fence and was hanging over into the water trough to play. He brought her to me, saying, "I think she wants to die!"

Three days after the car episode, as I was rocking her to sleep, my thoughts went to how that day could have been her funeral. I thought of the psalmist's words: "For he shall give his angels charge over thee, to keep thee in all thy ways" (Psalm 91:11 KJV). Tears of gratitude streamed down my face.

Little did we realize how often during the next year we would hold her tightly and thank God for sparing her. Or how, before the next year was gone, we would lay three tiny baby boys to rest. Three preemies, one born in November, and then twins in May.

We don't know how the Lord works, and it's not our job to figure it out. But we know that on that day, the angels must have been given a charge for Lori's safety. "The angel of the LORD encampeth round about them that fear him, and delivereth them" (Psalm 34:7 KJV).

Catherine

God's Protecting Hand

KATIE SHROCK

*R*obbers. What does that word bring to your mind? To me it brings back the memory of my family's terrifying experience in 1990.

It was a pleasant March night in southern Indiana. Most of the people in the little Rosebud village were sleeping peacefully, unaware of the danger lurking about.

But not all were sleeping. In the darkness, two men slipped stealthily down the road. Their hearts were beating fast as they approached Rosebud Country Store. If they thought about the all-seeing One in heaven, that did not stop them in their pursuits.

As dawn approached, the alarm clock started singing its merry tune in the bedroom of my parents, Glen and Pollyanna. Dad reached over and shut it off, wishing he could stay in bed a few more hours. But duties at the store called, and this was no time to sleep in.

When Dad walked into the store, his foggy mind did not notice anything amiss, until he went to get eggs in the cooler. The cooler door was ajar! "Why would someone leave the door open?" he wondered. Dad looked around, and suddenly he was wide awake. Flour, candy, and noodles were strewn around on the floor. Many items were missing from the shelves, the money box was gone, and the lock on the door was broken.

His mind reeled, trying to digest what he was seeing. Calming himself, he ran back to the house to break the news to the rest of the family.

"There were robbers in the store last night!" he said.

"No!" gasped Mom. "Surely not! What did they do? What did they take?"

We children gathered around, breathless, wide-eyed, and scared.

"Let's go out and see," Dad said.

We went out and surveyed the mess. The estimated loss was around $1,000. We weren't sure how our little store, which had just started up, would survive the loss, but we trusted God to provide.

* * *

In the next few days we tried to regain normalcy and have faith it wouldn't happen again. Precautions were taken: dead-bolts were put on the store's doors, and the money was taken into the house each evening.

One week later we were enjoying a quiet Saturday evening at home. Ed and Mary Slabaugh were our dinner and overnight guests. After supper was over and the children were in bed, the adults sat around, visiting and snacking. The dogs were restless and barked a lot. Maybe their thoughts kept returning to the robbers who had broken into the store a week earlier.

Dad and Ed went outside with flashlights to check it out. All seemed quiet, and they could not detect anything amiss. They committed everything into God's hands and soon settled into their beds for the night. It was around midnight, and it did not take long until all were sleeping soundly. The doors were unlocked, as usual, for we had no fear of prowlers in the house.

Suddenly Dad and Mom jerked awake, a breathless, panicky feeling enveloping them. Their bedroom door was swinging open, revealing two long-haired, masked men standing there with a gun pointed straight at the bed.

Surely it was just a dream, a horrible nightmare. But no—it was real! The men were in the room and coming toward the bed. The armed man came right up to the foot of the bed, and the other one stayed in the background.

A small kerosene lamp was turned on low on the nightstand beside the bed. "Blow that light out before I count to two!" the robber barked. Dad slowly obeyed, not wanting to make any fast moves. By now the man was right by Mom's feet, pointing the gun at Dad's head.

"Why did you report it to the police that we were here before?" the man with the gun asked.

Dad assured them they hadn't.

"Yes, you did, and that's why we're back."

Dad pleaded with them, "Please. Just take the money and go."

"Where's the rope?" they asked. "We never leave a job like this until the people are tied up."

The only ropes available were out in the barn, which made them quite upset. "Get us some sheets then," the leader demanded. My parents told them where the sheets were, and they got a few. "We're going to tie you and the old man up first. Now lie down on the floor!"

Mom's heart beat wildly. "No, no! They can't do this," she thought. "O Lord, please protect us," she breathed, wondering what they would do to her after Dad was tied up. This was the thought that made her tremble most. "Let's just pray," she whispered to Dad. Mom started softly crying.

Again the orders were given: "Get down on the floor!"

Suddenly Dad decided to call out to Ed. "Ed, die dieb sinn do!" (Ed, the thieves are here!) he yelled in Pennsylvania German. Then he repeated, "Ed! Thieves!"

The robbers became nervous. "What? Is there someone else in the house?" they asked. Then they began to hurry and strictly ordered Dad to get down on the floor.

At that point Dad and Mom both began praying out loud in English, pleading with God for protection and mercy. Obviously the robbers could not tolerate the praying. Making quick preparations to leave, the leader said, "Okay, we're going to go. We'll leave all your money and go."

Yet as they left, they grabbed the money bag, slammed the bedroom door, and shouted, "The first person out this door will die!" A motor quickly roared to life, and the squealing tires told of their departure.

An overwhelming feeling of relief enveloped Dad and Mom as they trembled and clutched each other in the darkness, weeping. Their hearts beat wildly. Were the robbers really gone?

Soon there were knocks on the bedroom door. "Who is it?" Dad asked tremulously. "Ed and Mary," came the reply.

They met each other with hugs, tears, and questions. Silently they went out into the rest of the house and viewed the mess. Cupboard doors stood open, canister sets were uncovered, drawers were opened, and some were emptied. The phone wire was cut through, and Bibles and books were lying open and scattered about. Wax drippings were on the floor, as the men had done all this by candlelight. It seemed as though they had tried to find money in every corner. My parents' and Ed's and Mary's faces were etched with shock. This was no nightmare; it was real.

Sleep was gone, even though it was only one forty-five in the morning. They sat down and shared stories. Ed and Mary had been sound asleep in their room when Mary awoke to the sound of rustling paper. First she thought it was a mouse. Then she decided it must be my mother, Pollyanna, up and doing something. But the continuing noises were mysterious enough that she got uneasy. Getting out of bed, Mary went to the door but did not open it. The sounds continued. She reached for the doorknob, but she couldn't bring herself to open it. Not knowing what to do, she went back to bed and tried to wake Ed. When she heard my father's call—"Ed, thieves!"—she doubled her efforts to awaken him. It was not until the motor roared to life that he finally woke up.

We children had slept through all of this. My sister Rose and I were sleeping on the hide-a-bed couch in the living room. The wax drippings went right past our bed. What were the robbers' thoughts as they looked down at the peacefully sleeping girls? Our guardian angels hovered near and kept us from waking to the robbery scene. We thought of the verse from the Psalms: "The angel of the LORD encampeth round about them that fear him, and delivereth them" (Psalm 34:7 KJV).

We attended church services that day. What a comfort it was to cry, pray, and share with our church family and to relax in their loving support.

Our neighbors contacted the police, and they came out that afternoon. The police were very disturbed, and they asked us to notify them if we found even the least clue of whom it might have been or if we heard of another attempt at burglary.

As the evening drew near, many apprehensive thoughts flooded our minds. Would the robbers be back? What might they decide to do to us?

So what a blessing it was for us to see a van driving into our driveway, carrying family from Ohio! They came to spend the night with us, because they knew that it would be a difficult night. Indeed, it was only after much praying and reading God's Word that we were able to sleep.

On Monday morning, our visitors left. With God's help we picked up the broken pieces of our hearts and tried to face life with courage and peace. But knowing the robbers were still on the loose gave us an uneasy feeling, and our trust was still to be sorely tested in the coming days.

* * *

Eleven days later, we again had overnight visitors. As bedtime drew nigh, the dogs were barking and raising a ruckus. Drawing the window shade, Mom thought she saw movement. She decided it was just her overactive imagination. After locking the doors, my parents went to bed.

But soon they heard someone at the door. "Oh no! Please, not again, Lord!" they breathed. Grabbing a bright flashlight, Dad went out and shined it through the window of the entrance door. One guy ducked and ran out the door. Dad and Mom decided to call the police. Then they went back to the bedroom to wait and pray.

Hearing another noise, Dad went out to investigate. Soon the beams of the flashlight revealed another man trying to hide in a corner. This man had a baseball bat in his hand. Seeing that he had been discovered, he came right up to the door. "I need help," he said, shaking his long unkempt hair out of his bleary eyes. "My car is stuck in the ditch."

"I think you need some other kind of help," Dad bravely replied. Dad talked with him some more, hoping he would stay until the police arrived. Finally, the man left.

Soon there was a knock at the door. It was a policeman with the news that they had caught both of the men. The robbers had been walking up the road when the policemen arrived. What a relief to know that, at least for the time being, they could do us no harm.

Once again, we were a very shaken family in the morning. Would we ever feel safe again? But time has a way of healing, and after a while, we no longer jumped at every little sound we heard after dark.

We are thankful to God for his miraculous protection over us as a family. We also praise God for proving himself faithful through the support and prayers of family and friends, which helped us through the difficult days that followed. We think often of the psalmist's words: "I will both lay me down in peace, and sleep: for thou, LORD, only makest me dwell in safety" (Psalm 4:8 KJV).

Katie

~ 23 ~

When You Put Your Money in God's Bank

DANIELLE BEILER

I start my minivan and watch the needle on the fuel gauge rise to only a little above the E. In the midst of rehearsing my day's lesson plans, I find myself calculating a real-world math problem: "Not quite a quarter tank. I should be good until Friday. I still have twelve dollars, so I can put a couple more gallons in for the weekend. If my check from church is in my mailbox Sunday, I think I'll just make it . . ."

My nearly empty wallet and fuel tank are uncomfortable aspects of a journey that began years ago. In the short drive to school, I review the events that have brought me to this place.

It all started when I was a junior in college. I was working on my biology education degree, living off my savings and cramming each day full of lectures, labs, and homework. Weekends were my only reprieve, and most Sundays I'd drive to the nearby town of Honey Brook, Pennsylvania, to pick some kids up for church. These children had become very dear to me. In my midtwenties and not even dating, I found that they gave me a little outlet for the mothering that wanted to well up in me. So Sundays I'd pick up four siblings and spend the day with them.

As we interacted, I began to notice some alarming gaps in the kids' education. The fifth grader could not read the Bible verses in Sunday school class. The second grader couldn't find the songs in the songbook because he didn't know his numbers. The girls, both in eighth grade, had a lot of stories of being bullied and of just generally not liking school. A seed of an idea began to grow in my mind. What if I offered to homeschool the kids for a year? Their mother had mentioned that she'd like to get them out of the public school, but she couldn't afford any other option.

I continued to play with this idea. I didn't like the thought of dropping out of college before I had my degree. And I knew this family would not be able to pay me a salary. But in the following months, God confirmed to me in many little ways that I was supposed to homeschool these kids, trusting him to work out all the details.

I had a few thousand dollars left in my carefully saved college fund, and I figured I would live on that as long as I could. I decided not to ask anyone to support me. If God owns the cattle on a thousand hills, he can take care of my needs, I reasoned.

Mom and Dad said I could put a schoolroom in their basement to get started. My excitement building, I began furniture shopping. I needed a table, some bookshelves, a cupboard for the kids' books, and a filing cabinet. About this time I got my first gift—a friend who had heard of my venture gave me a check for a couple of hundred dollars. I decided to designate this my furniture fund, but I soon found that even used furniture is quite expensive.

After much pricing around, I found an antique dining room table, a small cupboard, and a beat-up filing cabinet for good prices at a used furniture store. I bargained a little with the owner, and my final bill, with tax, was only pennies away from the amount of my friend's gift. I walked out of that store in awe. I had read lots of stories of things like that happening to missionaries, but experiencing it myself was a little mind-blowing. It really works, I thought to myself. Living by faith really works!

* * *

The basement classroom at my parents' house was not a good long-term option for our little school, and before long an opportunity miraculously opened up for me and the school to move to Honey Brook. Some men in the town owned a beautiful old stone house, and they wanted someone to live in it and use it for ministry. The living room, with its lavish trim and fireplace, became my schoolroom. I hung a slate chalkboard on the wall, put a wooden table in the middle of the room, and we were in business.

Soon after moving to town, I also found myself in need of a car. "What would you think about the Glicks' minivan?" my dad asked me. I tried to be polite in my response, but I was thinking I'd buy something more along the lines of a VW bug. Minivans were for soccer moms!

"Because if you want it, I would be willing to buy it for you," Dad continued.

"Yeah, I would be happy with that minivan," I said instantly. I mean, what could be more practical? And so I had a car.

I lived in the old stone house with a wonderful friend named Beth, and we had a blast furnishing its grandeur. Again, it took cash. Rugs, dishes, bedding, decor . . . not to mention food and toilet paper. A ministry in town paid our rent and utilities. I kept using my college fund, but it was dwindling.

One Sunday the deacon from my church asked me, "So who is paying you to teach these kids?"

"No one, really. But I'm sure God will take care of me," I said. He responded by taking my need to the church council, which in turn designated an open offering to go to my support. The Sunday of that offering, I turned around after the closing hymn and was shocked when I saw the offering amount posted in the back of the church. It was nearly $6,000.

Our church was small, and I didn't remember an offering ever coming close to that amount. Again, I had an overwhelming feeling of awe. I had chosen to trust God, and he was proving himself to me.

At the end of that first year, it seemed obvious that I should continue homeschooling. A friend of mine consented to join me as a teacher, and we added a couple of kids. We practiced math flashcards, read good books, took tons of field trips, and made hot lunch for the kids in my kitchen every school day. We cried a little, learned a lot, and experienced what it meant to be a beautiful little school family.

My church continued to support me, eventually committing a steady $600 a month. That allowed me to make some financial commitments, such as purchasing health insurance. I also got occasional gifts from family and friends to supplement my income, and lots of people donated money to the school so we could buy the supplies we needed.

In this season I decided not to lay aside any extra money I happened to receive but to give freely of what I had. I decided that God would be my bank. I would put all my money into his hands and trust him to return what I needed when I needed it.

It was a great concept, but God was about to stretch my faith through it.

* * *

As my second year of homeschooling turned into a third, and then a fourth, inflation and rising prices began pushing my cost of living higher. And then I hit a stretch without many gifts. It was in this season that I found myself watching my gas gauge every month, worrying that this would be the month that I would have to stay home because I didn't have what I needed.

I cringed when someone else used my toothpaste, because I didn't know if I could buy more. One night when I went out with my friends for frozen yogurt, I had to ask for a quarter so I could pay my bill. When I needed a gift for a wedding, I checked the thrift store and prayed for something that wouldn't look too used. Anything I really needed I quickly bought at the beginning of the month, because I knew I wouldn't be able to at the end.

I found myself questioning God in this season. He had limitless resources. Why did it seem he was being stingy? But I also found my desperate need pushed me to intimacy with God. I couldn't even shop without calling out to him. And I was gaining a tiny glimpse into what it was like to live in poverty, something many of my students had experienced their entire lives. (I don't pretend it was a very accurate glimpse—I still had my rent paid and lived in a lovely house.)

Fuel was the thing I worried about the most. My overall lack of funds was my little secret with God, but what would I do—and what would I say—if I couldn't use my van because the tank was empty? I knew there were people who would help me if I told them I needed help, but somehow God's provision

—without my asking people—was the sign I relied on that I was walking in his blessing. And so each month I worried and calculated.

After at least five months of nearly running out of fuel, I suddenly realized a remarkable thing: I was never quite running out. And so I made a conscious decision to stop worrying about it. God had my back. I would choose to believe that I never would run out. (I never have.)

I found in this season that although money seemed only to be trickling in, God had a million other ways to provide. About the time my minivan was wearing out, I got a text asking if the school would like a donated Honda minivan. The board of directors, which was now in place, elected to give me the Honda. When I needed a laptop, someone gave me an old one—and as it began to fail, someone else gave me a really sweet MacBook. Beth had a way of bringing home free stuff from the thrift store where she worked that was just what I needed—sandals that just needed a good washing, a dress with a small stain.

One spring I was facing pretty serious burnout. The school had grown to include five teachers and about fifteen students. We had moved to a church, which allowed us to use their facilities rent-free—another amazing gift. We had a board of directors. We had gotten our tax-exempt status as a nonprofit. We were a bona fide school instead of a homeschool. And I was trying to be an administrator, secretary, counselor, and teacher. I was exhausted.

At the urging of a friend, I applied to a Bible training school in Colorado. I sent in an application with more skepticism than hope. The cost for nine weeks was $4,000! After applying, I was almost angry with myself for daring to dream of going. There was no way I was going to be able to come up with that kind of money in the few months before the term began.

When the dean from the school called to tell me I had been accepted, I told her that I didn't know if she should plan on me because I didn't nearly have the money I needed to come. She told me to write a letter explaining my work at the school and my need. I wrote the letter.

A few weeks later, I sat at my computer reading an email and feeling that holy weakness that washes over me sometimes when God shocks me with his goodness. I could go to the Bible training school. Someone had paid my tuition, and someone else was opening her home to me so I could live off-campus for very little rent.

So I flew out to Colorado for an amazing, rejuvenating summer. Partway through the summer I felt God urging me to give most of my money to someone else. So I walked to a bank, filled an envelope with cash, and slipped it into the correct mailbox at the school. Small problem: I hadn't calculated very carefully how much money I had, and now I realized I didn't have enough left to pay my rent.

God had that covered, of course. My birthday brought a few cards with a little cash, and my rent was paid on time.

* * *

I am now seven years into this journey. This year I am taking a sabbatical from teaching and I am enrolled again at Millersville University to finish my bachelor's degree. I need thousands of dollars before fall for everything to stay on track, but sometimes I almost forget to pray it will come in. I've put my money in God's bank, and I trust him to release the funds that I need when I need them.

"Bring the full tithe," God tells Israel in Malachi 3:10 (ESV). "Thereby put me to the test . . . if I will not open the windows of heaven for you and pour down for you a blessing until there is no more need." I have tested God, and he has indeed poured out his blessings.

God has also tested me. He has pushed my faith, stretched it. He has asked me to laugh at the impossible and to expect the miraculous, to give generously even in my own need. And perhaps most beautiful of all, God has taught me that he not only watches the sparrow, but knows when my fuel gauge hovers near E.

Danielle

Zippy

SHERRY GORE

P.U.! The car smells really bad, Mom. Even worse than before!"

"I know," I said with concern. "I can smell it too. Zippy isn't going to last one more mile if I don't get off the interstate soon. Thankfully, I just saw a sign that showed there's a truck stop just ahead. God has protected us so far, and he isn't about to leave us stranded now. Let's keep singing."

"Lord prepare me . . . to be a sanctuary" rang out louder, perhaps, than we would normally sing in the car. My three children (then ages eleven, ten, and six) and I were determined to not let discouragement take over amid an already difficult situation.

It was Thanksgiving Day, and we were making the eight-hundred-mile drive south to our hometown of Sarasota, Florida. Zippy was the name my children gave our new-to-us car: a green 1974 Buick Apollo that had cost me $500. Someone had recently borrowed and totaled our family car.

We had recently found ourselves in a new and potentially frightening situation, and I needed to sit down with someone I trusted to get advice on what the four of us should do next. The bishop at our home church was just the person to visit, so we were headed there in our Buick Apollo.

But now Zippy was starting to jerk and go slower than it should have, considering my foot was pressed down hard on the gas pedal. One of the children had left our gas cap at a station while filling up the tank earlier in the journey. I would pump the gas the next time, I decided, and see if the station had a spare gas cap. The gas tank was nearing empty now, but I knew that this was a mechanical problem, and not something even a full tank could fix.

As I steered the car toward the exit ramp, the engine quit. I prayed out loud for protection and assistance as the car continued rolling. Surprisingly, it stopped directly in front of a Pilot truck stop in southern Georgia. We were some three hundred miles from our destination.

"Stay put," I told the children as I climbed out of the car. "But keep praying." With gas prices at a seemingly all-time low, I had exactly the right amount of money in my purse to get us to Sarasota and back—but not a dollar more. I certainly would not have enough to even begin to pay for car repairs.

Within seconds of getting out of the car, I noticed a man making his way across the parking lot to us. He had a long beard and was wearing broadfall trousers and suspenders. While his face wasn't familiar, his appearance was—clearly he was Mennonite. Relief washed over me.

"I think God sent me here to help you," he blurted out.

I was taken aback by his words, but I told him, "Well, I've been praying for help. We all have, at the first sign of car trouble about four hours ago, sir."

Later I would learn that Troy (not his real name) had recently begun attending a Mennonite church in New York. He was a long-distance trucker, and he had delivered his last load of supplies three days earlier. Now he had returned to the truck stop to wait for the call directing his next pickup order. Sitting there at the truck stop for three long days without a single call was frustrating to him, and it was something that had never happened before.

He shared with us how he had prayed during those three days, "Lord, what is it? Why are you making me wait here when I could be out driving, earning money for my family back home?" This was to have been his last trip on the road. Next week he would begin working from home full-time as a carpenter so he could spend more time with his family.

After brief introductions, he told me to take the children into a sandwich shop in the truck stop to wait while he took a look at my car. Not long after, he entered the restaurant and stood next to our table. "It's not something I can fix, so I called to have the car towed to a local garage," he said. "It's not open today, because it's a holiday, but at least we can get it off the road. Are you all hungry?"

Without waiting for an answer, he pushed a twenty-dollar bill in my hand and said, "Here, order yourselves some sandwiches. I've got a call to make. I'll be back. I'm going to call my wife to tell her why God made me wait here all this time. It was to help you."

* * *

Funny as it may sound, we enjoyed those sandwiches immensely. It wasn't the Thanksgiving dinner we were looking forward to, but we were truly thankful in our hearts. God had been seeing to the details of our lives before the crisis even occurred.

I wasn't sure what to do next. The little bit of money I had would only get us the rest of the way. That left forty-five dollars to get us back home again.

After we ate, the children and I prayed together for guidance and a roof over our heads. Would we stay here, in the noisy truck stop? What would we do?

Troy came back inside and said, "I've secured a room for you at a hotel nearby. If you're ready to go, I'll take you there."

More moments of trust on our part. And thankfulness.

We climbed into the semi cab and within minutes were dropped off as promised, at the Red Roof Inn. It was nice, clean, and comfortable. More thankfulness.

The next day, Troy returned to pick us up and drove us to a nearby shopping center. "You can window-shop here while you're waiting for your car to be fixed. Here's the number to the garage. Call the mechanic in two hours to see if he's finished." He also told us his boss had called. There was a load offer—a good one, too. For the first time, he told his boss, "No, I'll have to pass it up." He wasn't willing to leave until he knew we were safely on our way.

I still didn't know how I was going to pay for the repair. I didn't tell the children. I kept praying.

Two hours later, the mechanic told me, "No, ma'am, I'm still working on it. Call back in an hour."

I don't think there was another item to be looked at in any of the stores when the day was done. Every hour, for the next four, I called and heard those same words again, until the last call. "I'm not sure I can fix it, ma'am. You may have to junk the car. Come in an hour. I'll be done whether it's fixed or not."

One hour later we walked to the garage and found the only mechanic in sight sitting behind a desk. He was the garage owner too. I stood there, not sure what was coming next.

"Well, I got your car fixed," he said. With his head cocked to the side a bit, he told me, "I don't know why, but I can't charge you for the repairs. Something just keeps telling me not to.

Gotta listen to strong feelings like that, ya know? I do, however, have to charge you for the tow. I don't own the tow truck."

He paused. "That'll be forty-five dollars total, ma'am." Forty-five dollars was all I had in my purse, not counting the twenty-dollar bill it would take to get the rest of the way to Florida.

I was so grateful to the mechanic, and I wished I had something of value to give him. Something—anything at all—to show our appreciation. Then I remembered the peaches in the trunk of the car. They were the finest peaches you can find: Baby Golds. I had canned them earlier in the year, and they were the last two jars left. I had brought them along on the trip to share with my bishop, to show my appreciation to him.

But instead, I gladly set the golden-colored jars on the mechanic's desk. "I wish I had something more to show my thanks, sir. But it's all I have," I said, as I tried to hold the tears back.

"I'm right thankful for them peaches, ma'am," he answered back, smiling. "Been a long time since I've had anything to eat that looked so good."

I shook his hand first, and each of the children did too. My heart was overwhelmed, and with tear-filled eyes I turned back at the door, to say goodbye, and saw tears on the man's face too. "Happy Thanksgiving," we each told him. "And thank you for everything!"

The four of us practically bounced into the car. After starting the engine, I glanced at the fuel gauge. It was on full. "That's funny," I said aloud. "The car was just nearing empty when we broke down. That man must have filled our tank! What a wonderful thing to do!"

My little son jumped out and opened the gas tank door. "Mom, you're not gonna believe this, but he even put a shiny new gas cap on!" More tears of happiness.

Just then we watched as Troy pulled up in the parking lot and got out of his rig. "I see everything worked out for you all," he said. "I'm glad. And I just took a call from my boss. He thought I was crazy yesterday when I passed up the load to haul. But he had a better offer today, a bigger load, and it pays almost twice as much as I'm used to. This is my last run before heading home for good. I just never expected it to be so faith-stretching."

We said our goodbyes and pointed Zippy southward. We didn't know what lay ahead for the four of us. But we did know we weren't going alone. We just had to keep trusting God.

Sherrey

V KINDRED

You know who will stick with you when the chips are down?" my dad would ask me when I was a teenager sitting slumped in the back seat of the station wagon on my way to yet another boring family gathering. "Family! Relatives! That's who!"

The reference to gambling was ironic, coming from a guy who wouldn't even play bingo. But my dad's refrain about the importance of family was etched into him. As a Russian Mennonite refugee and immigrant, my dad had lost so many family members to war and tyranny, including his twin sister, Anna, when they were just ten months old. Thus, any excuse at all to be with family members was all-important to him for the rest of his life. Now I get it. And I wish with all my heart I could time-travel to that station wagon, headed for a warm home filled with a father, grandparents, aunts, and uncles who are no longer here. Because family—kin—is important.

Those relationships are weighty, no matter how difficult and painful they sometimes are.

In the following stories, women write about their relationships with family.

"When we have opportunity, we should take part in family reunions," writes Gertrude Slabach. "If we listen closely, we'll hear stories rustling among the branches [of our family trees]." (That may be my favorite line in the entire book.) These writings explore different permutations of family, starting with the musings of a young mother, at home with her little ones, for whom she makes untold sacrifices. "Salty ones," Melissa Troyer writes. "I've tasted the tears."

One woman writes about the disconnect between herself and her mother-in-law, very different people trying to understand each other. And in a narrative that fascinated me, an Amish grandma reminisces about her own grandfather, and the time his rebuke led to her losing possession of a cherished doll.

Perhaps the story most kindred to my heart is "Ground-Laid Eggs" by Mae Unruh, a Russian Mennonite like myself. Mae remembers the hospitality extended to her by her great-aunt. For Mae, those visits bonded the generations and passed the torch of story and heritage. She recalls with relish the lofty angel food cake made only with "ground-laid eggs" as being the fluffiest she had ever eaten. And she remembers hearing the language of Platt, or Low German, being spoken around her. It was a language she could understand but not speak. Reading her account took me back to my own childhood and visiting Grandma Loewen's farm. There I could understand the gist of a conversation spoken in Platt. *There the cakes were always fluffy and perfect.*

Hopefully these writings underscore my dad's motto: Family sticks with you, even when the chips are down.

Laurel

~ 25 ~

The Way of a Man

SHEILA PETRE

*W*e were both eighteen when I saw him at a singing. I stood in the back with the other young women. The ushers filled empty benches where they could, and they asked Michael to sit far in the front of the church building, in what we call "the amen corner." I didn't think him particularly handsome—his hair was dark blond and curly. My dad, whom I did consider handsome, had straight hair, coal black at the time.

But there was a certain unease about this young man—a sense of being out of place with so many others and yet an aura of being complete within himself—that drew my attention again and again to him. He looked a bit sulky, as I told my mom later. She was dismayed that such a look would appeal to me. After that, when I told the story, I learned to say that he looked as though he had lost his best friend. Aha. Or maybe she hadn't shown up yet.

That was the first time I remember seeing him. My older sister taught his grade-school brother, whose hair was curlier and cut shorter. Through her, I heard bits about his family, and about the family dog, Whiskers. I remembered meeting his mother some years earlier, and her warm friendliness to a young woman she scarcely knew.

I was eighteen and a half when I shattered my nose against a tractor trailer in a vehicle accident that also totaled our minivan, partially collapsed my lung, fractured my eye socket, and broke my younger brother's leg. The accident also propelled our family, briefly, into after-church discussions across our community. My older sister took the brunt of our disrupted family life, hurrying home from school to help, distracted by the beginning of her own courtship. She carried tales of our accident, and updates on our healing, to school. A curly-haired student of hers toted the stories home to his family's supper table, where his older brother listened.

I had to stay home from work and church for several weeks, perhaps months, after the accident. When I finally returned to singings and church services and Bible study evenings, he was there, more and more often, at the congregations I attended. He wore glasses when he drove, with dark plastic frames that did not become him—cheap glasses, probably, because his parents are frugal, a trait I am grateful that they instilled in him. During weekly Bible study services that winter, I sat across from him, near the front of the same church where I had seen him first.

It was there that I first noticed his hands. They weren't . . . clean. Some of his fingernails were cracked, and they were stained black, as were the creases of his knuckles. "Mechanic's hands," someone said—but he wasn't a mechanic. He was a welder, I had learned, and he used those hands hard, assembling stair railings or tearing tractors apart, unafraid of grease. His hands were also scarred—and still are—marred by flying sparks and slipping grinders. He is a fabricator, a word I found in a small, admiring profile his younger sister wrote about him for the school newspaper.

"A *fabricator!*" said my brothers. "You can't trust his word!"

This was after I had discovered Michael's sidelong glance upon me several times, often enough to nurture a small crush. Or perhaps not so small. When I came home from work on the Friday after my nineteenth birthday, I found an envelope from Claylick Road with the stack of birthday cards on the fridge. I knew whom it was from.

I opened the envelope and took out the embossed pink birthday card—and had never before felt so feminine, so courted, so awed. His brief note asked me if he could have the "priviledge" of my friendship. Not even the auxiliary *d* diminished my amazement that someone I scarcely knew would consider my friendship a privilege.

A month and six days later, on a fine June Sunday, I stood at our front door and saw him come up the walk to meet me. I wondered whether this was real, and why I had never noticed before that he was, well, a little bow-legged. He was also still awkward, still out of place, and still not quite as handsome as I would later realize he was.

As for our courtship, it was a realm consisting mostly of words, and I excelled at those. I'd been waiting all my teen years for an opportunity to write love letters, and I did so, filling a book with them, not confident enough in our relationship to give them to him directly. Oh, to be sure, he could use words too, and did so. On a walk on Clopper Road on a crisp fall evening, sixteen months into our courtship, forgetting the way he had written his request for my friendship, he asked if he could have the PRIVILEGE of being my husband. This time he let me spell the word as I wished to, which is why I write it here in capital letters.

I told him yes.

* * *

We were married on a rainy day in April, and then we set out on our wedding trip. It was then I discovered that while he may have been clumsy at courtship and I at ease, I would be clumsy at marriage and he as careful, confident, and sensitive as though he had been born for it. We visited Niagara Falls, Corning Glass, Pathway Publishers, and an emergency room in Vermont, where I was diagnosed with an ear infection— something I do not, as a rule, recommend for a honeymoon. But he proved his wedding vows early—in sickness he was as compassionate as in health.

By the time we returned home, two-and-a-half weeks later, his fingers were no longer stained under the nails or in the cracks of his palms—for the first time since I had known him, and for the last. Within days he was again carrying the evidence of his livelihood in the creases of his hands.

That summer, in a caravan of vehicles packed with belongings, we helped my parents move across the country to Washington State. He drove one vehicle the whole way west, and we flew back home a week later. I don't remember much of those first months. In the mornings, we cuddled in the corner of our not-yet-furnished living room to share devotions, reading aloud from Song of Solomon (what Christian newlywed couple doesn't?). We stretched his lunch break to the limits of its allotted hour, and in the evenings, we read late, each of us deep in our own books. It's hard to believe that we had almost ten months of being only two. He fulfilled his wedding vows throughout that first year: during my loneliness for my family, my ineptitude in the garden, and twenty pounds of weight loss and forty pounds of gain, and through my morning sickness and a long, exhausting labor.

With the birth of our first baby, he proved his superiority all over again. I bumble at parenthood, but he's a natural. He woke at night with our daughter when I was too exhausted, begged to take her in church, and—of course—was the first to sneak her bites of table food.

Then there was the second child, and the third. The first learned to talk and walk, and she'd run to the door and call out a loud, "Daddy home!"

"Oh," I say now, when people look again into my children's faces and share a comment or two, "I tell my husband that's why I married him: I knew he would have cute babies." Or I share the impetus God used to draw my husband's attention to me: "What girl wouldn't break her nose to catch a husband?"

But away from others, waiting for his eager step at our door; serving him his favorite bean soup and sausage for supper, or the thick heel of homemade bread; watching him let his children push him down the stairs to their shrieks and his pretend panic; listening to him talk to God about me; crying in his arms for no reason at all and every reason I can think of; passing a random building in town and hearing him explain how he helped make the handrail for it, or passing a truckload of strange steel beasts on the interstate and holding my breath lest he wreck while he cranes to see and tells me those are parts for a horizontal boring machine: in all these glimpses of who he is, I know the answers are not so simple. Why was my attention drawn to him, in particular? Why did he choose to court, love, and marry me? God led us together, as surely as he sculpted those skillful hands and that sensitive mind and as surely as he bent those legs and curled that hair.

I think of the phrase in Proverbs 30:19, about the fourth thing too wonderful for even the wisest on earth: "the way of a man with a maid" (KJV). With Solomon, I confess my inability to comprehend the mystery. I just thank God that Michael is the man and that I can be his maid.

Sheila

The Kingdom Here in Our Arms

MELISSA TROYER

I rolled over and turned off my beeping alarm. Soft morning light drifted in the window, and despite the fact that it was Saturday, I shook my husband's shoulder. "Wake up, honey. It's six."

We are not morning people, especially not my six-year-old son. I knelt over him and whispered, "Remember the race? Gotta get ready." His eyes flew open. It was surprisingly cool for a morning in late May, and as we crawled out of our car at the park, I wished I had brought a sweater. The runners lined up for registration, pinned on their numbers, and warmed up their legs.

A tall man pushed a jogging stroller to the line, and I noticed his son was special, very special. The signs of Down syndrome were clear, and I knew I would have to meet this little guy.

I knelt in front of him, smiling into his sleepy face. "Nick isn't much of a morning person," his daddy said, smiling.

"Hey, I know the feeling . . ." I looked into little Nick's sky-blue eyes and rested my hand on his knee. "I'm gonna be cheering for you, Nick!" He smiled faintly and nodded, his blond hair glowing in the morning light.

The horn went off, and my husband started the race, along with the throng of other runners flooded out onto the track. Nick's dad held back until there was a bit more room and joined the tail end of the group. Nick leaned back into the stroller and settled in for the ride.

It was a perfect morning for a run. I bounced my eight-month-old baby and chatted with the others who were waiting to cheer the returning runners. I kept scanning the track, and finally I heard someone say, "Here comes the first runner!"

Sure enough, here came that thin guy, wearing all black, with that beautiful stride. My man.

The little girl in me came alive, and I bounced over to the finish line. "Come on, honey! You're amazing!" My husband came flying in, beating his previous race record by several seconds.

More and more runners came through: my sisters, a cousin, and a friend. I cheered for each one of them. But I kept looking for that blue jogging stroller. I knew Nick and his dad would be near the back, since they had started out last. And finally little Nick came around the bend, his sweaty dad pushing that familiar stroller. The finish line filled with people, and we waved and cheered. "Good job, Nick! You did it!"

Here I was, screaming my heart out for a kid I'd never met until today. And he was all smiles.

A few minutes later, the race officials handed out the medals. One by one, the best times and names were called. And for his age group, Nick got the second-best time. He crawled out of the stroller and ran up to the medal table. As he was handed the red ribbon and the shiny medal, a huge smile spread over his face.

Instead of going back to his seat, Nick twirled the medal high over his head and danced around the pavilion. The crowd cheered. We laughed. Nick's eyes glittered and his face glowed. Tears stung my eyes. We all watched this little guy dance in sheer delight, and we all tasted heaven.

* * *

I had to think about the story in Matthew 19 in which Jesus is teaching and healing the thronging masses. Everywhere he and his disciples went, people were pressing, shoving, reaching for that healing touch. Then came the children, full of energy and mischief, brought by eager mothers.

I can just imagine the disciples' exhaustion as they begin to intervene: "Not today. No, not these kids . . ." But Jesus pulled the children close, and he looked reprovingly at the disciples, "Let the little children come to me and do not hinder them, for to such belongs the kingdom of heaven" (Matthew 19:14 ESV). He touched them. He held them close. He blessed them. He saw their worth. The kingdom of heaven. Jesus himself taught us to pray: "Our Father in heaven, hallowed be your name. Your kingdom come, your will be done, on earth as it is in heaven" (Matthew 6:9-10 ESV).

God's kingdom, here on earth. It's a breathtaking thought. No sin. No grief. No loss. No sadness. I saw it, there after the race, as Nick danced and jumped on legs that wouldn't straighten perfectly. He limped, in fact. But he was jumping for joy with sheer delight that was marred by nothing.

The kingdom of heaven is not far away. For us mothers, it is right here in our arms.

I had no idea when my first child was born that he was sent from God to teach me. The mother was now the student. This child, who could do nothing for himself, was an instrument in God's gentle hands to teach me about myself and my Maker.

I learned about rest as my baby slept so soundly in my arms.

I learned about trust as I cradled my son in the shade by that roaring riverside, waiting for the body of my brother to surface after his drowning accident.

I learned about complete dependency, as I was the only one who could comfort my child when he was hurt.

I learned that holding him was comforting to me, even in those moments when I didn't realize I needed comfort.

Now that my children are a bit older, I'm learning the vital importance of honesty—of telling them that I messed up, again. I am amazed at how quickly they forgive, and I find my breath taken away again by these little teachers.

It's so easy to miss. Children are a gift. A miracle. An opportunity to see life through pure and untainted little eyes. "Mommy, look!" My daughter bends down over a teeny-tiny purple flower I hadn't even noticed.

I pause. Here in the stopping, in the learning to see, the embracing of a new perspective, we get to taste life in its sweetness.

Life as it was meant to be.

It only takes one trip to the store to be reminded that motherhood is such a huge chore. "My," people say, "you have your hands *full.*" I only have three little ones in my cart. I smile back, "Oh, we have lots of fun!" They look at me oddly. But it's true. We are embracing today, with all its joys and trials, for today is a gift.

Oh, I know. It *is* hard.

Pregnancy is not a walk in the park. And birth? Wow. The teething baby won't be settled, the challenging attitudes and the outright disobedience need to be faced. We aren't able to go on dates as we used to, or even join the prison choir that we helped start, because you can't take a nursing baby behind bars. These are sacrifices. Salty ones. I've tasted the tears.

But this calling of motherhood is the invitation to experience God's kingdom on earth. To choose to dive into the beauty of today. To be intentional about taking time to look deep into these little eyes, these windows of heaven. To see. To listen to their hearts, and to build towers of colorful blocks and relationships that will last through adolescence and hard questions.

And it's about joy. It doesn't just happen. As mothers, we mold and shape the way our children will think about themselves and the world around them. We can create a negative atmosphere, nagging and discontented, by wishing for the next season, a better house, or more perfect and comfortable circumstances. We can subconsciously teach our children to live for themselves, selfishly wanting everyone to cater to their needs. It's terribly easy. Because it's what feels good, here and now.

But you know what? Life isn't about us. Sounds cold, I know. But honestly, my life is just a speck in eternity. One wave that comes crashing onto the shore, in and then out and forever gone.

Let's look at ourselves through God's eyes. Let's see today the way he does. Meet those hard moments with a thankful heart that says, "God, I thank you for what you want to teach me through this." Not only will you find your heart more at rest; you will notice the sun shines brighter.

You have traded the temporal for the eternal. You will be shattered. You will have hard days. Your children will see you cry. You will need tissues and burp cloths and diapers, pacifiers and cardboard books and moments alone in the bathroom (just for those two seconds of solitude). Those long hours of uninterrupted reading or journaling will give way to snack time and Legos, to teaching simple addition and coloring inside the lines. But instead of resenting your children's ever-presentness, celebrate the opportunities that these little people create.

As the book of James says so well, "Count these moments of testing as opportunities for joy. For you know that after you have chosen to walk through it with a joyful heart, God will work unwavering faith deep in you. And as God perfects it in you, through these days of sacrifice, you will be made perfect and complete" (James 1:2-4, author's translation).

You will lack nothing, here in this place of agreeing with God and embracing today.

Pull your little ones close, smell their hair, and feel the warmth of their skin. Catch the sparkle in their eyes. Laugh deep and hard with them.

Look up and smile. God has sent these beautiful little teachers into your life. Grasp their small hands, and dance to the beat in your heart.

Can't you hear it, that heavenly song? The birds, the wind, and the glittering creek, and you and your children together join in that beautiful melody of God's kingdom here on earth.

It is the most beautiful place to be.

Melissa

~ 21 ~

Stories Rustling in the Branches

GERTRUDE SLABACH

*I*t wasn't that much fun back then. Each autumn, we were sent out to the pasture to gather hickory nuts. Although encased in a large outer shell, the nut itself is small. Do you know how many nuts it takes to measure one cup of chopped nutmeat for a recipe? A lot!

Sometimes we fussed and complained, but we went nonetheless. It was autumn. Hickory nut cake was the cake that our mama liked best, and it was almost time for her birthday. So we went.

It became a tradition and part of who we were as siblings and as a family. That frosting—with brown sugar, real butter, and heavy cream—was a pure taste of toffee and maple sweetness. Oh what bliss!

Now when I taste this cake and this frosting, I am a child again, back in the warm kitchen with my family. It's dark and wintry cold outside, but there is warmth in the kitchen, and I belong.

Many years later, two cousins and I traveled to the land from which our great-grandfather Wilhelm set sail when he left Germany at the age of fifteen. We walked the streets of the small town of Langendorf, and we imagined that the cows wearing cowbells were descendants of the cows our forebears had pastured 150 years before! My cousins and I imagined that we saw distant relatives in the faces of folks we passed on the street. Pensively, we stood by the lot where the Bender house had been. There was something about being among these people that felt like home.

When we returned home to the United States, our mothers and aunts enjoyed the stories of our travels and our descriptions of that geography across the Atlantic, so like the homeland of their own childhoods in Pennsylvania. The photo taken of the death record of Wilhelm's father, who was buried just days before the remainder of the family left Germany, prompted somberness. We regaled our family with tales of the town their grandfather lived in before his journey to America.

"On Sunday morning," we told them, "all the women were out sweeping their porches and sidewalks, just like you do here."

Their eyes twinkled when we said, "We couldn't get away from our mothers even though we were an ocean apart!"

It's true. There are some things about family that are special just because that's who we are. Often there are traits and characteristics that we don't even recognize as belonging to our families. Yet there is familiarity in being part of the folks we call family. We develop traditions without even realizing we are developing them. Something done once is repeated the next year, and the next year . . . and suddenly it's an unplanned tradition.

Your family might not claim hickory nut cake as a novelty, but you can likely name things that are special and that belong to you just because you are a family. Tracing the path back to the beginnings of a tradition can help you identify and claim your roots. When we have opportunity, we should take part in family reunions. If we listen closely, we'll hear stories rustling among the branches that we had no idea were there.

Go back home and find the place where you belong. Going back home can sometimes be painful, but we still need to go. Memories of insecurities are bound to surface. You might find yourself reverting to the child you once were. Other adults might still view you as the bossy older sibling, the complacent middle child, or the spoiled baby of the family.

Yes, our family trees can be warped and gnarled, but it's who we are. We are family nonetheless.

It helps sometimes to go back and find out why we do things the way we do. It's not so much that our way is better than someone else's; it's just that learning why we do the things we do will help us understand who we are.

A cousin of mine moved with his wife and small child to the basement of his parents' home for the summer. They were in transition between jobs, and he wanted to go back home for a few months so his wife could learn to know his community better. He also wanted to reconnect with folks he hadn't been able to spend time with for several years.

At the end of the summer, his wife told me, "I learned to know my husband so much better by being around his family. I never could understand why Nate always walked around the kitchen eating his cereal and kicking the cupboard doors shut with his feet. It used to drive me crazy. This summer, it finally made sense. His dad walks around the kitchen, eating his cereal, doing the exact same thing. Now I understand!"

As individuals in a family, we are significant because we belong. Whether we're part of the tree from our beginning or whether we were grafted in, we belong. We not only belong to the tree; the tree is a part of us.

Those knots and gnarled limbs? There's a story behind them. We should listen to those stories. Hearing them will help us learn to know our past, and it will help us understand our present.

It's true that we didn't have a choice in the decisions made by our ancestors. Yet, we can choose to change the course of our future by how we respond to our past. One of the best ways to begin is to understand those who are part of our family and its tree. To do that, we must climb the tree.

By acknowledging this tree and its gnarled warts, we can relish its shade. We can change, if necessary, its bent. We can lean toward the shadow or toward the sun. The direction we lean will plot the course of our future tree. We can allow the past to cripple or empower us. We can choose life, thus setting the course for future generations. That's what God meant when he said through Moses, "This day I call the heavens and the earth as witnesses against you that I have set before you life and death, blessings and curses. Now choose life, so that you and your children may live" (Deuteronomy 30:19 NIV).

* * *

Just a few weeks ago, a cousin stopped in overnight on her way back home. I asked her if she had ever made the frosting for the hickory nut cake recipe that is in the *Mennonite Community Cookbook.*

"Oh yes," she said. "I'd be happy to make my mama's cake and frosting again."

I thought to myself, *Your* mama's cake? It's *my* mama's cake! After all, my mama's birthday was in November, and I had been certain that no other children anywhere were ever sent out to the woods or pastures to gather hickory nuts. How wrong I was.

When I began asking around, I found out that first cousins from nearly all my mother's siblings confirmed that their parent also liked hickory nut cake. They shared memories of gathering nuts and then sitting outside on large stones and cracking those tiny nuts using another rock.

"It was always important," one cousin recalled, "to be sure to get the nut out in an entire piece."

"We tried our best to get the half out without breaking it so we could put a circle of nuts around the outside of the top layer of the cake," another cousin said.

Well now. That could have been spoken by any of my siblings—or any other cousin, for that matter. So all these years, my sisters and I thought this recipe was special because our mama liked it. Now we know that our grandma loved nut cake first. Small wonder, then, that her offspring claimed hickory nut cake as a favorite! This tradition had been passed down without any of us being aware of it. Yes, the hickory nut doesn't fall far from the tree.

So go ahead. Recognize the roots of your tree. Run your hands along the bark of the trunk, and feel its solidness. Embrace the limbs. Climb that tree, and rest against its branches. Understanding where you come from will help you recognize why you are and who you are. It will also help you evaluate where you want to go and who you want to become. That family tree? Claim it. Embrace it. Then choose life.

gertrude

Still Ourselves—Just a Lot More

DORCAS SMUCKER

Five years ago today I delivered a baby goat.

Facebook reminded me this morning; otherwise I would have thought it happened much longer ago. So much has happened since then. But I still remember as if it just happened this morning.

I had once again left my family and boarded a plane in Portland, Oregon, to fly to Minnesota to rescue Mom and Dad from a crisis. None of my family thought they should still be living on the farm on their own at eighty-nine and ninety-four years of age. But they disagreed, and we did things their way, which tells you a lot about my parents.

This time Dad had been in the hospital with an intestinal blockage. He was back home but still tottery and too frail to walk to the barn to do his chores. "I'd like you to check the nanny goat," he said. "She's due to go into labor any day now."

On my third check, I heard the goat bleating desperately before I even got to the barn. I rushed in, turned on the light, and hurried to the pen. She was standing there calling for help in that deep, helpless, frustrated way that only a woman who's been through a tough labor really knows. I felt a rush of empathy.

I'm sure my husband or my dad would have said, "Let's give her some time." But the way she bleated and looked at me, well, I wasn't going to wait.

"Hang on. I'm coming, sister!" I thought as I opened the gate, stepped into the pen, and got to work. A little nose was out, and two little hooves. I broke the slimy sac and started pulling, first one hoof, then the other, then the rest of the head.

I waited a bit, and the baby didn't move. Thankfully, an ear flicked, so I knew it was alive. I pulled a bit more. When a human baby's head and shoulders are out, the rest comes slipping out with no more trouble. Not with this baby.

I pulled it out farther, about halfway, and waited for the nanny to push. She still couldn't move it. So I slowly pulled the rest of it out and laid it on the straw: a big, beautiful, black-and-white mass of goat and slime and glop.

The nanny's relief was immediate, and I could empathize with that too. She turned around and started licking the back of her baby. I grabbed a handful of straw and began working on the nose and mouth, cleaning and scraping. Soon, with a series of snorts and shakes and sneezes, the baby came alive.

The mom just licked and licked, relieved and happy and full of love.

It was amazing. I stood there in the shadowy barn and tried to take in what had just happened. The pride, the joy, the wonder, the miracle of birth.

Then, as the curious barn cats came by and peered between the slats of the fence to see for themselves, I wiped my sticky hands on straw, pulled my phone from my pocket, sent exultant texts to my family, and took dark, blurry pictures.

I thought I really should go to the cafeteria and bring the nanny some tea and toast, the way the nurses had done for me when I had a baby in the middle of the night. But the nanny had plenty of hay and water, so I left it at that.

Today, I think about how much things have changed since then. My mom is in heaven, and my dad lives contentedly in an apartment in my brother's house. I can plan trips to Minnesota a couple of times a year, at my convenience, rather than dropping everything every few months to fly back and rescue them, leaving makeshift and chaos in my wake here at home.

When I was in the middle of that season, it was overwhelming and difficult, and I thought it would never end. Sometimes I cried and begged God to please just let me stay home for a while.

When the time was right, it ended, and I survived. Now my young adult children can easily run the house when I'm gone.

Tending to that laboring nanny goat had transported me twenty years back, when I was in the middle of the baby years. In their own way, those years were even tougher and more challenging than the aging-parent years. The baby years, however, fill me with nostalgia, and at night I often dream I have a baby again.

Deep in the demands of a particular season, we think it will never end. It goes on and on—sometimes full of joy we want to clutch with our hands and never let go, and sometimes with suffering that seems it will never pass.

The truth is, every era comes to an end. As each stage begins, and again when it ends, the question we face, inevitably and frighteningly, is, Who am I now?

Crazy was the word we used for ourselves, back in my youth group days. Crazy was good, it was fun, it meant you had a life even if you lived in the middle of Minnesota. Crazy was slumber parties where you laughed until the wee hours and snuck off to shaving-cream Daniel's car when he and Clara had their first date—and their only one, which was probably our fault. Crazy.

My sister Margaret and I would ratchet up the craziness when we went shopping, especially at garage sales, such as the time we found both a huge teddy bear and a little wooden potty chair at the same garage sale. We sat the bear on the chair and went out the driveway, collapsing into the car and screaming with laughter. And then we realized we had plopped into the wrong car.

Then I got married, which shook my sense of self, because now I would always be not just me but this man's wife. Pregnancy, with its months of ghastly sickness, reduced me to a miserable shell of myself in both body and spirit. Whoever I had been, I no longer was, and, I feared, would never be again.

What I didn't see until much later was that God creates us as unique individuals, precious in his sight. He does not send these challenging new phases to eradicate who we were and make us into a hollow, sad new person. Instead, each stage, tough as it may be, adds a layer of wisdom and beauty to that deep-inside personality.

We are still "us," only a lot more so—better and wiser, more empathetic and insightful, less fearful and selfish.

The teenage me would have seen a laboring goat as gross, or maybe as a scientific curiosity to be observed at arm's length. The forty-eight-year-old me took charge. I wasn't afraid or repulsed. I had the courage and wisdom of hard-won experience. I could feel deeply and also act decisively.

At a recent writers' conference, I marveled at the wave of young Anabaptist women writers coming along. They are talented and connected, on their way to great things. I felt suddenly old, as though they were passing me by.

"You are not a has-been!" insisted the two young writers I confided in. "If we are coming behind you, it's because you have blazed a trail worth telling."

Of course. That pattern once again—time passes, an era seems to be ending, and the frightening question emerges: Who am I now? And: Am I done being me?

Still you, the Father assures. Just a little wiser, a bit more experienced, with new assignments still ahead.

And sometimes we get to go back and enjoy a taste of who we were back then. A year ago, my sisters and I went shopping in a secondhand store in Pennsylvania. Unnoticed, we sidled up to one another's carts and slipped in wild gold sandals with six-inch heels, unspeakably garish purple undergarments, and similarly silly specimens, then casually wandered off again.

Up at the checkout, we found the additions in our carts and shook with laughter as if we were fifteen again.

The three of us have supported each other through the teenage years, the college-and-job years, marriage, young motherhood, sickness, grief, and now mothering young adults. The first wedding among our children is coming up in May. Most of the time, we are responsible women who have been through hard seasons and come out better on the other side.

But deep down we are still us, still who we always were, still who the Father created us to be, still a little bit crazy.

Dorcas

~ 29 ~

Remains of the Doll

BARBARA FISHER

*T*he glory of young men is their strength: and the beauty of old men is the grey head" (Proverbs 20:29 KJV).

I find this Bible verse rather amusing, but let's stop and think. There is a truth in it. Sure, the glory of young men is their strength, and the young women look up to their husbands who have all this extra strength. But when this strength starts to diminish? That's when men actually get their special beauty.

I remember my grandfather Jacob Esch. He was the jeweler of Intercourse, Pennsylvania. He was born in 1869 and lived to be ninety years old. When he passed away, I was thirteen years old. I rather adored him, and I secretly hoped I would someday get to be ninety years old too. He had a full head of beautiful white hair, with not a bare spot on the top of his head. He passed this treasure on to his two sons and many of his descendants. My six brothers all have a share in it. If you meet an elderly man with a big woolly head of white hair, it may well be my brother or cousin.

But my grandfather passed on more good treasures than just his white hair. He was a man with strong morals, and strong beliefs of right and wrong. I still admire him for these things—even though he was the reason I had to part with my most beloved doll.

* * *

When I was a little girl, we had some chickens on the farm, and sold some of the eggs to local customers. An old school friend of my mother's would come every week for eggs, and we would always sit on the porch and visit awhile.

One evening she brought a doll along and asked Mother if we could have it. It was an old, used one, but it had real hair. My mother did not approve of the hair, but she was sure she could take it off. Sure enough, the hair was just glued on, and underneath were nice markings of hair such as most dolls have. The doll had a hard plastic head with eyes that closed. Mother painted the hair black and the lips red. It was a large doll, and it could fit in clothing the size of a newborn.

My older sister made a dress and apron and a covering for my new doll. Of course she didn't make the clothes quite as old-fashioned as Mother would have made them, but they weren't fancy, either. Just right, I thought, and I was utterly thrilled. Love was written all over my face, and I was in sheer glory. You see, I had only had one doll before this.

Along comes Grandpa Esch one evening to visit. He and Dad were visiting in a circle of guests, and I was right in the midst of them, playing with my beloved doll. I don't remember if my grandpa asked about my doll, but I do remember setting her up right in the middle of the floor and saying to everyone, "Now doesn't she look real? We can even make her sit by herself."

Well, after we children went to bed that night, Grandpa told Mother he didn't think we should have that doll. I realize now that it looked to him as though I was worshiping it as an idol. In some ways, I guess I was.

But what amazes me now is that my mother took the advice of her father-in-law. The next day she nicely told my sister and me that Grandpa didn't think we should have the doll. She did not tell us how hard it was for her to tell us, but I know it was.

I can still feel my shoulders slumping in disappointment. I don't remember that I even tried to beg, but I was sad, very sad. My mother went right to work and took the doll apart. She destroyed the stuffed body, but she said she would not destroy the head, arms, and legs right away. She tucked them away in a closet in her bedroom. I remember going in to look at it sometimes. I still wonder to this day whatever became of it. Evidently as I got older, the remains of the doll disappeared.

How many mothers would respect their father-in-law to this extent? In fact, I think I would be guilty of avoiding this myself. But did it hurt me in the long run? I don't think so. I believe it was probably a good lesson in giving up and growing up.

I managed not to lose respect for my grandfather. His advice actually made me feel that he was the real, all-knowing grandpa, ranking next to God.

By the way, this makes me think of my dad, who also had a full head of almost-white hair. One evening after my husband and I had church here at our house, my parents were here and stayed overnight with us. We had just gotten our new Bible story set. That evening our son Gideon Jr., probably about four years old at the time, asked, "Who would be oldest: grandfather or Abraham?"

Honor thy father and thy mother, we learn in the Ten Commandments—and, I would like to add, teach your children to respect their grandfathers and grandmothers. "Children's children are the crown of old men; and the glory of children are their fathers" (Proverbs 17:6 KJV).

So the next time you find a few gray hairs on your head, don't fret or sigh. Say, "Thank you, Lord, for sharing with me such beauty. I may even yet get to be real pretty!"

Barbara

~ 30 ~

The Perfect
Mother-in-Law

DENISE SHANK

I have the perfect mother-in-law," Karen announced one
day at a quilting.

Instantly, I was all ears. Someone had a perfect mother-in-law?
How remarkable! A perfect mother-in-law. How could it be? I
had ceased to believe that such a person could exist. And now, to
suddenly discover that my good friend, Karen, was claiming that
her mother-in-law was perfect . . . why, it was quite a discovery!

My own dear husband's mother was far from perfect. There
was no doubt about that. And her imperfections seemed to rub
me the wrong way. She was a petite little lady who always ran
through the work at hand. She'd have a half day's work finished
while I was still putting on my shoes. There was nothing wrong
with her being able to work, but did she always have to be brag-
ging to me about what all she accomplished?

Take yesterday, for instance. My day began on the wrong
note, and I couldn't sing a bit. The baby was sick and thus had

the grumps. I couldn't do anything to keep him happy, and nothing else seemed to go right either.

After supper, Mom clipped in the door with a fresh strawberry pie. "What all did you get done today?" she asked in her brisk way.

I felt my face warm up as I watched her eyes sweep across my cluttered kitchen. "Joshua is teething," I murmured in embarrassment. "He took up most of my day."

"Oh, that's too bad," she sympathized. "When my children were grumpy, I put them to bed with some toys and they learned to play happily themselves. I didn't have time to baby them."

"Of course you didn't have time!" I wanted to shout at her. All my poor husband remembers of his mother is her being busy, busy, busy. No time for stories, or games, or anything fun. "And guess what?" I wanted to add. "You grumble that your children don't confide in you! And just why do you think they don't? It's because you never gave them time to feel comfortable talking to you! When they wanted to tell you their childish troubles, you brushed them off. Yes, I know you were too busy to baby your children. You don't even have to tell me that."

But no, I did not say any of these things aloud. I kept them all to myself. I was still trying to think of some suitable way to reply. Something nice and meek sounding.

But Mom was already speaking again. That was another area in which she was always a step ahead of me. She could be through her first paragraph while I was still trying to think of an opening sentence. "Joshua looks happy enough now," she said. "Why don't I just stay and help you clean up your kitchen while he's being good?"

I wanted to tell Mom that we had other plans. Daniel had told me that we were going to bed early that night and that he would help me with the messy kitchen in the morning. But how could I tell her that? She was already getting hot water to wash the dishes. I looked helplessly toward Daniel, but he was busy scratching figures at his desk and seemed totally unaware of what was happening.

With an inaudible sigh, I began clearing the table. It was true: Joshua was happily kicking his feet and gurgling in delight. But why wouldn't he be? His big sister, Linda, was booing at him and entertaining him to his heart's content. And two-year-old Abigail was sitting happily on Daniel's lap, watching him figure. Yes, all the ducks were in line for Mom and me to finish cleaning up the kitchen in short order.

"I got my garden all cleaned up today," Mom said as she splashed the dishes. "It was terribly weedy. Have you seen it lately?" she wondered.

"No, I guess we have not been past for a while," I answered.

"It was terribly weedy," she repeated. "And you know, I planted ten pounds of peas this year so that I can sell some at Matthew's roadside stand. So it sure took me a while to get them weeded all by myself. I sure was tired when I was done."

"I guess you were," I said. "I wish we could have helped you ..." With my three small children, I knew that helping her would have been impossible. Still, I thought, it would have been a nice thing to do. Vaguely, I wondered if there ever would come a time when Mom would even truly need help with anything. She could manage everything, it seemed. I almost thought she could even manage to tell God that he was not supposed to let her live a single day after she was too old to work.

"You help me weed my peas?" Mom looked at me with wide-eyed horror. "That would be awful. You have enough to do the way it is. No, don't you even think of helping me! Why, your own peas are in dire need of help. Actually, I think yours are weedier than mine!"

Again, embarrassment coursed through me. Why had I bothered to mention that I thought it would be nice to help Mom? What a dumb thing to think, let alone say.

Anyway, our kitchen was back to good order within fifteen minutes. Daniel closed his checkbook and surveyed the transformation. "Looks better," he said. "Thanks for your help, Mom. I was planning to help Denise clean the place up tomorrow morning." He grinned. "Now I won't have to."

Mom was horrified. "Daniel! You have enough to do without helping your wife in the kitchen! All those cows to take care of. Whew, I sure am glad I stopped in this evening."

She turned to me. "Look, anytime you get in a pinch just let me know. I'll be glad to help you. Daniel is busy enough." She shook her head. "Dad never had time to help me in the kitchen when we were young farmers. I didn't want him to, either. That was something I could take care of myself."

I felt like a very old, worn-out dishrag until Mom left. I could do nothing right. Mom could do everything right. All I did was make a fool of myself.

* * *

Daniel understood my feelings. This was by no means the first time that Mom had treated me this way. The discouraging part was that I knew it would not be the last time, either. "Don't worry about Mom," Daniel comforted me. "Just let her talk and don't worry about it. I know that you did the best you could today. And God knows it too. That is really all that matters."

I was grateful for Daniel's sympathy. But it did not take away my discouragement. Would I ever be able to do anything right for my mother-in-law? I longed for a good relationship with Mom. Yet every time we were together, I was left feeling hurt.

Back when Daniel and I had been dating, I had such nice ideals about mother- and daughter-in-law relationships. I would always treat Mom with respect. I would do and say things that she would like, and I would make her happy. She would be so glad that Daniel had chosen me for his wife. She would share little things with me about how Daniel did this or that cute thing when he was little. We would feel a kinship, because she was the mother of this wonderful man and I was his wife. A perfect relationship. A perfect mother-in-law.

Those dreams had been shattered during the first week of our marriage, and I had never managed to pick up the fragments. I spent a lot of time pondering mothers-in-law and daughters-in-law and relationships.

And so it was that my ears perked up at Karen's announcement at our quilting. A perfect mother-in-law! How exciting. I wondered what her husband's mom was like. Kind. Quiet. Caring. Soft-spoken. All these words were chasing each other through my mind, one after another. I waited for Karen to continue.

"Yes, I have a perfect mother-in-law," she repeated. Then she paused, as if to make sure that fact had soaked in for all of us.

Only then did she continue. "At least, my mother-in-law thinks she is the perfect mother-in-law."

Plunk. Karen's announcement had the effect that she had anticipated. Our visions of Karen's mother-in-law were instantly altered. I groaned within myself.

I broke off my thoughts because Karen was speaking again. "Mom can do everything right. At least she thinks she can. And I have two ways of thinking about her and I can't decide which way of thinking is the best."

"What are they?" I asked.

She grinned. "Well, sometimes I am just plain mad at her. She can get so much more done than I can. At least it seems like she can. And I feel mad."

Karen paused. "Then sometimes I am jealous of her. She can manage everything. Her life is all perfectly ordered, and everything works out just like she plans. My life seems to go here and there, and just fizzles out."

"Actually," Karen continued, "I know that neither feeling is right, and I am working on letting God help me to straighten out my feelings."

I was quiet. Jealous? Karen was jealous of her mother-in-law? How could she be jealous of the mother-in-law who thought she was perfect? Impossible, right?

Jealous. Could I be jealous of my mother-in-law? Of course not. Why would I be jealous of her?

Then I remembered Mom's petite form. I was large and clumsy. Mom's movements were smooth and graceful. Efficient. Was I jealous of Mom's efficiency?

Maybe I was. I wanted to have my peas all weeded and my kitchen spick-and-span. I wanted to help Daniel in the barn and still have time to stay caught up with all my work. I accused Mom of not caring enough about her children. But deep inside, I wished that Joshua would happily play in his bed with toys for a while so that I could do half a day's work before he was ready for his shoes.

Maybe I was even jealous of the way Mom could talk. When I had company, I had to struggle to begin a sentence. I was not an interesting person to visit with, and I knew it. When Mom had company, no one was bored by her intriguing paragraphs.

Jealous? It was a new thought to me.

* * *

I discussed it with Daniel that night after the children were in bed. "I know that I have been mad at Mom already," I said. "But I never thought about that maybe I am jealous of her."

I paused. "The more I think about it, though, the more I believe that is part of the reason that I . . . that I have trouble appreciating her."

I drew a deep breath. "I wish life could click along as nicely for me as it does for Mom. And when it doesn't, I get upset at Mom! I am really not being fair to her, am I?"

Daniel ran his hand through his hair thoughtfully. "I think you have a point. We have both probably been jealous of Mom already. But remember, you are doing some things for our children that Mom never did for me. You take time to nurture our children's souls. I would rather that you continue to be the kind wife and mother that you are being, even if that means that our garden is not as clean as Mom's."

My heart warmed at Daniel's high and undeserved praise. But my mind fogged. I wanted to have better feelings toward Mom. What help toward that goal was Daniel's praise? Even the realization that I was jealous of Mom—what did it benefit me?

But Daniel was not finished talking. "As far as our jealousy over Mom's accomplishments—well, I think we need to get rid of the jealousy. At the same time, maybe it would be good if we dwelled more on the things we are jealous of."

"Whatever do you mean?" I wondered in bewilderment.

"Just that," he said. "You wish your kitchen stayed as orderly as Mom's. What if Mom's kitchen was always a mess, and she never had time to help you with anything either? Do you think you would like her any better that way?"

It was a different way of looking at things than my usual run of thoughts. I *did* appreciate the results of Mom's help. It was merely her way of making me feel like a failure that caused the hard feelings.

"I do like her helpfulness," I began slowly. "But . . . but why does she always manage to say such unkind things? And . . . and . . ." I couldn't think how to finish my sentence.

Daniel was smiling. "It's because she is not a perfect mother-in-law," he said gently. "We both enjoy her good points. Can we expect her to be perfect in everything when we are not perfect ourselves?"

I slowly nodded my head. Then I remembered that I should be shaking it instead.

"Mom really does love us in her own way," Daniel reminded me. "She does not have a tactful way of showing her love, but she cares about us. If she didn't, she would never bother to wash our dirty dishes. And I know she makes you feel like a poor excuse. But she never goes around telling people anything bad about you, does she?"

"No," I said with warmth. "I have always appreciated that about her. She keeps my faults and failures to herself." Even as I was saying it, my head was drooping in embarrassment. How many times had Daniel and I discussed Mom's faults? And yet when was the last time we had paused to remember her good points?

"I want to do better at appreciating Mom," I murmured.

Daniel nodded in understanding. "I do too," he said simply. "You know, I chose you for my wife because I wanted a woman who would mother our children better than Mom had mothered her children." He squeezed my hand with affection. "But that doesn't mean that it's right for us to hate Mom just because she isn't perfect."

I smiled in agreement. "And it's not right for me to be jealous of her either, just because she is not a perfect mother-in-law."

After all, I reminded myself, there was no perfect mother-in-law to be found on this earth. If Mom were to have all the lovely qualities that I longed for in a mother-in-law, then there was sure to be something else about her that would be less than ideal. That is just life. God expects us to strive toward perfection, but he has not promised us attainment until we reach heaven.

I determined that, with God's help and Daniel's reminders, I would quit dwelling on Mom's ability to make me feel as though I could do nothing right and she could do everything right. Or as Karen put it, I would forget that I had a mother-in-law who thought she was the perfect mother-in-law. I would focus on the good things about Mom—such as her helpfulness and her interesting stories.

I would harbor no wrong thoughts even when she managed to weed her whole garden and make five strawberry pies while I was still floundering around to find my lost shoe. And when she shared paragraphs about her accomplishments with me, I would smile cheerfully and never utter a sentence.

From here on out, I would ask God to help me appreciate my imperfect mother-in-law.

Denise

Ground-Laid Eggs

Mae Unruh

My father's widowed aunt and five of her daughters lived in the neighboring county. Dad's old gray '37 Ford (and later the dark blue '46 Hudson, a four-door sedan) often cruised down the country road toward that county to visit her and her children. My father often took the mile east of the county road when he drove "up north"; that road seemed less bumpy thanks to less traffic, and he was not a slow driver.

On our way to visit my dad's relatives, we'd take notice of the farmland and crops along the way. In that county I recognized several landmarks signifying we'd soon be there. One was the white Lone Tree church my father's relatives attended, and another was the graveyard where my mother's parents were buried.

We usually arrived unannounced at my great-aunt's house, unless it was by special invitation, maybe for a dinner. My father's aunt and her deceased husband were parents to seven children. Two children, one son and one daughter, were married. The other five daughters, including a set of twins, lived with their widowed mother and ran the farm.

When Father stopped the car in the well-kept farmyard, one of his cousins was soon at the outside porch door, walking toward my parents to greet them with a handshake and a greeting in Low German, also known as *Platt*, a dialect of some Russian Mennonites. Then the conversation would continue in Low German, which I could understand but not speak.

While my parents visited inside the large, white, two-story farmhouse, built around 1902, I would roam the farmyard. My great-aunt's daughters each had their own duties, chores to which they attended day in and day out. Some did cattle chores and milking; others took care of the poultry. Another was the cook, and another the gardener. The girls farmed and drove the tractor, but the harvesting was done by neighbors.

There would be cows in the corral or in the pasture adjoining the barnyard. The family had sheep and sometimes, if our visits occurred at the right time in the season, lambs. The chicken houses had hens, a poultry house had pullets, and the family also operated a hatchery. My great-aunt and her daughters had a lot of fowl: turkey, duck, geese, guinea, some bantam hens, and setting hens with little chicks. They also had dogs, and barn cats that, over the years, became house cats. We loved to hear Dad's cousins relate their encounters with the farm animals. The twins, especially, were animal lovers, giving names to all their farm animals. Some of their animals even understood *Platt*!

My father's aunt had a massive garden from which she and the girls dug bushels of potatoes and canned ample amounts of vegetables, supplying them well until the next year. Surrounding the vegetable garden was the flower garden, and throughout the front yard perennial flowers bloomed in abundance and profusion.

When we were invited for a dinner, the table was spread out in the big dining room, laden with scrumptious food prepared from scratch. I cannot recall any menus, but one table item—the woodpecker toothpick holder—was indelibly engraved in my preschool mind. You would press the woodpecker's head into a basket that looked like a tree trunk, and the woodpecker's beak would pick up a toothpick.

One year while vacationing I entered a gift shop and saw a woodpecker toothpick holder very much like the one in my memory. I bought it. I hope the little children in my extended family will have memories of my toothpick holder too!

My dad's cousins were all excellent cooks and bakers. They often served their company goose or duck. They tried new recipes and served the delicacies using their pretty dishes. They made cakes, pies, and breads as special orders and delivered them to neighbors.

Dad's cousins were also talkers, with each sister having something to say. If one failed to relate how the event occurred, the others were adept at filling in the missing links—in great detail.

One day when we were visiting, their story was about the angel food cake we were eating, which had been made with "ground-laid eggs." Believe me, those angel food cakes were made from scratch and mixed by hand in their small kitchen. My generation cannot recall using a wire whisk to whip egg whites until stiff, but that's what they did. And those cakes were absolutely perfect in texture, and they rose high above the baking tin!

So someone asked them, "What do you mean by 'ground-laid eggs'?"

"Ground-laid eggs?" they said, as if they couldn't believe someone would not know what they are. Ground-laid eggs, we learned, are the eggs that are laid on the ground or in the soil in the chicken yard and not in a nest.

Now, I grew up on the farm, and our hens always laid eggs in nests. Occasionally we'd find an egg on the ground the first week or so after the young pullets had been moved into the chicken barn. But we'd never have enough fresh ground-laid eggs to make an angel food cake!

I still don't really understand how those ground-laid eggs were of such a superior quality. I mean, an egg is an egg, whether laid in the nest or on the ground, right? The only thing I can figure is that a ground-laid egg cools faster on the ground than one laid in a nest of straw—maybe that difference in the raw egg is beneficial for high-rise angel food cakes. Or maybe it is the method they used to make the angel food cake: the love that was added to the mix as the egg whites were beat and the batter deftly stirred.

After the meal, my parents would visit with my great-aunt in the parlor, where an assortment of antique chairs, rockers, love seats, and bookcases lined the walls. Before the visit was completed, the girls would ask their guests to help sing some German hymns, and then they'd ask my father to have prayer before leaving.

I marveled at those young women's abilities, and their stamina, as they worked like men on their farm. Over the years, as they began aging, the hardships of toil did eventually slow down their lifestyle. But for many years, even as they grew older, they kept making those magnificent high-rise angel food cakes with ground-laid eggs.

Mae

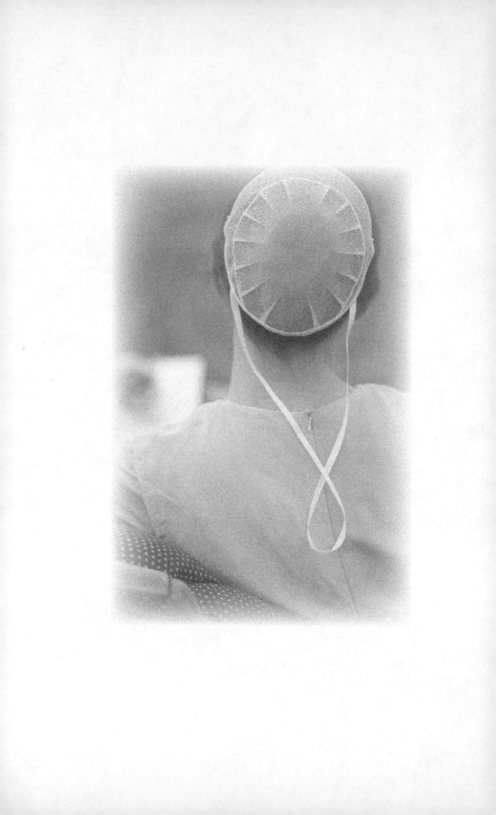

VI BELOVED

*B*eloved: adored, cherished, treasured, dearly loved. *Do we believe that we are beloved in God's eyes? As I gathered these stories, I expected to be engaged, to smile and smirk, to be held in the power of a good story. But I didn't expect to be stirred in the hidden places of my spirit. I didn't expect to be drawn closer to the One who calls me (and you) "beloved."*

In order to draw closer and know just how cherished we are, we have to learn that God is our sufficiency. "I . . . must recognize that I am inadequate," writes Rae Schrock. "I do not have what it takes—to save a life, cancel an emotional debt, be a kind person, or cope with ministry challenges. Admitting my brokenness gives God room to work."

Many people feel their most alone at Christmastime, when we are "supposed" to be filled with nothing but cheer and sprinkles. As Lauren Stolzfoos so tenderly writes, *our weary hearts may not always feel like rejoic-ing. Yet there is hope: "He will heal. Joy is around the corner. Redemption is nigh," she says. "And isn't that what Christmas is all about? Redemption. Jesus came to redeem; that's his chief business. He wants to take the hard things of life and make them into something beauti-ful. He wants to take your hard holiday and turn it into something beautiful." (If you're closer to Easter right now, don't miss Lucinda Miller's powerful piece "Jesus, Who Lives in the Mud.")*

Finally, I soaked in Samantha Trenkamp's musings on shame in "Rebuilding from the Shambles of Shame": "We feel shame . . . and so we must go to the Lord for healing and affirmation. The ugly becomes beautiful, the wound gives way to health, the shame gives birth to life lived in sweet abandon to a loving Father." A loving Father who wants us to know we are kept and loved.

~ *32* ~

The Lord Is My
Sufficiency

RAE SCHROCK

esus, I need you.

These words have been playing on repeat in my head for the last fourteen months. All my life I have been aware that I need Jesus, but the past year and a half has opened a whole new understanding of how dependent I am on him. Even on my best days, I am fraught with inadequacy. I pass up opportunities to show love. I say hasty words. I entertain critical thoughts. On my own, I do not have what it takes to, as Ann Voskamp says, "do this one life well." Yet I praise God! Although the events of the past year have revealed my deep and startling limitations, they have also unveiled to me the completeness of Christ's sufficiency.

This past year, I made a big life transition by moving from my home of seventeen years to a new community. Living far from family and lifelong friends has been more difficult than I anticipated. I came with expectations of a seamless transition and of doing this "transplanting thing" just right. So I was shocked when, instead, I felt bowled over by the adjustments. I dreaded going to work at the God-gifted job I had moved for. Making new friends turned out to be really tough. My whole identity felt rearranged, and in the emotional upheaval of change, loneliness often kept me home, hiding in my room and wishing someone would come find me.

The thing about life, though, is that it doesn't wait for us. I had to get up and keep going to work, paying bills, and managing a magazine. Many days I felt so emotionally raw that I could barely find the physical energy for my daily tasks.

In the past, I had met life's troubles with the support of close friends and my own mental toughness. This past year, though, those sentinels of strength were stripped from my life. I learned to reach out to Jesus more vulnerably than I ever have before. In the absence of people and situations to ease or distract me from the burdens, I learned to lay my heart before the Lord, telling him my troubles and crying out to him for help.

"Jesus, I need you!" became, and continues to be, my prayer. He heard my cries, and answered, often in the form of Scriptural promises: "I know your heart's desires and will satisfy them. You are my beloved. If you walk with me, no harm with come to you. I will turn your night of sorrow into the morning of joy" (see Psalm 37:4; Mark 1:11; Psalm 91:1-10; 30:5). Affirmations of God's good heart toward me brought hope.

Many days I experienced a supernatural strength that carried me through long days and tough decisions. Moment by moment, God encouraged my heart and brought rest, where before I had been consumed by anxiety. It became clear to me that grace is for the present moment: not tonight, or tomorrow, or next month. It is for *now*, and it is fashioned to fit my unique need.

I think we often feel that grace would be better if it came in larger swaths. It seems it would be easier to lean on Jesus if we had long-term guarantees rather than the call to trust him moment by moment by moment. Yet this is what keeps us near God's heart. Being in situations that make us acutely aware of our deficiencies is what keeps us continually depending on him. It is the place where growth happens, and where his power is most felt.

Growing into new seasons of life calls for new kinds of dependence on Jesus. This is how life should be. To become fully mature in the faith, we must encounter new limitations so that we might also discover new aspects of Christ's sufficiency on our behalf.

Several months ago I was hired as the nurse manager of a faith-based crisis pregnancy center. There I have the extraordinary privilege of caring for women with unwanted pregnancies, ministering to their physical needs while also caring for their emotional and spiritual injuries. Many of these women come with heartbreaking stories. For women who are already struggling with difficult and complex life situations, an unexpected pregnancy can be devastating. Never before have I felt that my words and actions carry so much weight. If a baby's life is on the line, reaching the mother's heart is imperative.

A few weeks ago, a client sat in my office and told me she wanted an abortion. She told of the recent death of her fiancé, the father of her four children, and of how afterward she'd had a breakdown and lost her youngest child to the state. Bitterly, she explained that the father of this baby was already out of the picture, incapable of taking care of himself, let alone her and a child. She had no money, no job, and no car, and she was shut out by her family. Whatever faith she once possessed had been buried beneath an avalanche of pain and loss. Having a baby now was just too overwhelming.

Everything I could think of to say sounded horribly trite. Her pain was deeper than any I have ever experienced, and her current situation was complex and difficult. I made some kind comments, but they felt shallow and dissonant with the deeper needs of her heart. I felt lost in my big office chair, wondering why God would call me, a sheltered little Mennonite girl, to a ministry in which I would be caught at a loss for words.

Maybe you feel this way too, sometimes, in the tasks to which God has called you: mothering, marital struggle, relating to a lost friend, coping with long years of singleness. Paul's words in 2 Corinthians express exactly the inadequacy I felt in that moment: "For we are the aroma of Christ to God among those who are being saved and among those who are perishing, to one a fragrance from death to death, to the other a fragrance from life to life. Who is sufficient for these things?" (2 Corinthians 2:15-16 ESV). Being entrusted with the truth is heavy. A lot of times I feel too clumsy to wield it properly.

But then I remember the rock of truth behind every believer's mysterious strength, and the stunning answer Paul gives to his own question: "Not that we are sufficient in ourselves to claim anything as coming from us, but our sufficiency is from God, who has made us sufficient to be ministers of a new covenant, not of the letter but of the Spirit" (2 Corinthians 3:5-6 ESV).

These words must be some of the most powerful declarations in Scripture. They hit me like a splash of water, awakening my heart. Yes! I am sufficient because Christ lives in me! He is the Savior, and I am his vessel. I am not called to save lives but to show Christ. If my primary agenda is preventing an abortion, then the plan is easily thwarted; my work is in vain. But if my chief goal is to share Jesus' love, then nothing can interfere.

In that conversation with my client, the oppressing fear—of saying the wrong thing or missing the perfect opportunity—

lifted. The words of the Holy Spirit simply came: "Jesus loves you so much. He cares about what you have been through, and he wants to bring you healing." The woman began to cry, her strong demeanor crumbling as the tender presence of Jesus touched her heart. It was a sweet and unexpected moment.

The next day, my client returned for an ultrasound. There were more tears as she glimpsed her baby for the first time, marveled at its miniature perfection, saw its tiny heartbeat. This precious lady chose life that day. Her decision was not because I was so eloquent or so smart but because Jesus used me in my weakness to serve as a vessel of his love.

This was a powerful lesson in my life. How many times do I get in the way of the Holy Spirit by believing I have to do his job? Do I really think God needs my great strength and wisdom to accomplish his plans? There is something freeing about letting God be God. It frees the tongue, releases supernatural wisdom, and empowers me with strength I could never possess on my own. When I stop defying my innate human inadequacy and instead hold it up as an offering to God, his sufficiency becomes mine.

There is no shame in admitting our innate weakness to God. In fact, it is those weaknesses—physical or emotional—that qualify us to receive God's power. This is the reverse economy of the kingdom: in Christ the poor are made rich, the weak are made strong, and the humble are lifted up. It is good for me to understand my human insufficiencies. They keep me humbled and calibrated to the reality of who God is. As I experience my own weakness, I am exposed to his sweet grace, a gift I could not receive if I was not in need. My inadequacy reveals Christ's sufficiency.

Setting aside my self-strivings to depend fully on God is a process. I often wrestle with how to apply the concept practically to my daily life. This story from 2 Kings has been meaningful in my journey:

> The wife of a man from the company of the prophets cried out to Elisha, "Your servant my husband is dead, and you know that he revered the LORD. But now his creditor is coming to take my two boys as his slaves."
>
> Elisha replied to her, "How can I help you? Tell me, what do you have in your house?"
>
> "Your servant has nothing there at all," she said, "except a small jar of olive oil."
>
> Elisha said, "Go around and ask all your neighbors for empty jars. Don't ask for just a few. Then go inside and shut the door behind you and your sons. Pour oil into all the jars, and as each is filled, put it to one side."
>
> She left him and shut the door behind her and her sons. They brought the jars to her and she kept pouring. When all the jars were full, she said to her son, "Bring me another one."
>
> But he replied, "There is not a jar left." Then the oil stopped flowing.
>
> She went and told the man of God, and he said, "Go, sell the oil and pay your debts. You and your sons can live on what is left." (2 Kings 4:1-7 NIV)

This story captivates me. We read of a woman who is, in every way, at the end of her rope. Her husband and provider is dead. Her sons are about to be taken as slaves to settle her debts. This woman has no other options; she is destitute, and she knows it. Here is the first lesson about claiming God's sufficiency: I, like the widow in this story, must recognize that I am inadequate. I do not have what it takes—to save a life, cancel an emotional debt, be a kind person, or cope with ministry challenges. Admitting my brokenness gives God room to work.

Stubbornly insisting that I am capable dams up his grace and leads to spiritual destitution.

Like the widow, we need to know whom to ask for help. This woman recognized Elisha as a man who could help her, and she went boldly to him. Even the strongest people in our lives aren't enough to shore up the weakest parts of our souls. We need something more to equip us for our daily tasks. In my own life, I am learning to run to God first with my needs—great or small—crying, "Jesus, I need you!" Time spent with him brings wisdom and solace that no human being or circumstance can.

I love Elisha's response to this woman's plea for help: "What do you have in your house?" She first answered, "I have nothing there at all," and then added, "except a small jar of oil." It must have seemed almost ridiculous to mention something so small. Yet it was this small flask of oil that multiplied to buy her sons' freedom.

We might ask ourselves the question, What do I have in my house? Our smallest, most unlikely resource—even the thing we deem a weakness—may be the thing that God intends to multiply into the fulfillment of our needs. Stop and take inventory. Look in the corners of your heart and life and see what resources of time, money, talent, and wisdom you have available. Then take those resources and, as the widow did, put them to use.

Elisha instructed her: "Go borrow empty jars from all your neighbors. Don't ask for a just few. Then, go into your house, close the door, and fill the jars." What an astonishing command! It might have sounded irrational to this woman, but she obeyed. She prepared for abundance without any rock-solid guarantees that it would come. Yet she was obedient to Elisha's command and gathered every available receptacle. Her faith was miraculously rewarded.

As I've pondered this story afresh, I have been amazed to realize that the number of jars she gathered determined the amount of provision she received. Scripture tells us that the oil stopped multiplying as soon as the last jar was full. What if she had only borrowed two? The oil would have stopped flowing when the jars were full, and the income generated would not have been sufficient to pay off her debts. This is sobering to me. God invites me to test him—to offer up my meager flask of oil and see if he won't fill every empty jar I can get my hands on. Yet my faith is often shortsighted, and when I find myself in need, I stop collecting at two.

God is calling you and me to borrow empty jars and to prepare for abundant provision. Stepping out in faith is scary. But like a muscle, faith grows strong with practice. I encourage you to begin with small steps. Today, do something that requires faith: start a life-giving conversation with a stranger. Share your testimony in church. Enforce that new daily routine your kids will hate but you know they need. Be honest with a friend. When we ask God to come through for us and then prepare for plenty, we communicate our love to him. He invites us to trust him completely, and promises to abundantly respond: "I am the LORD your God, who brought you up out of the land of Egypt. Open your mouth wide, and I will fill it" (Psalm 81:10 ESV). The degree to which I trust God is the degree to which I will experience his sufficiency.

The Lord has been my sufficiency over and over again. When I come up empty, I cry to him for help, and he hears me. The strength, wisdom, and courage that result are as miraculous as the widow's provision of oil. I want to be more like her: freely confessing my need, asking for help, and then preparing for plenty.

Like the small village child who came with many thousands to hear Jesus, I have nothing to offer him save a few loaves and fishes. They will never be enough to meet my needs or the needs of those around me. So I will give them to Jesus. He will multiply my meager offering to feed multitudes and to fill me as well.

Rachel

I Would Sell Everything
and Buy a Field

LUCINDA J. MILLER

When I was a little girl, nighttime shadows were large around me, and I imagined spirits and demons against the wall. Bible passages and revival meeting preachers had painted vivid pictures in my mind of the horrors of hell, and I was afraid of dying and going there. I did not know how to be a Christian, and I was afraid to ask. Lonely and terrified, I cried myself to sleep many nights.

And then one day I gathered courage. I talked to my mom and dad, and I did what they told me. I prayed and asked God to forgive my sins and take me to heaven when I died.

The fear was gone. And God was close—so close that, lying on my back on my bed, I could have reached up and touched him—but even that cannot describe his closeness. He was next to my heart. I felt that he loved me, and this surprised me. Puny Luci Miller, nine years old, inadequate and fearful—and this God of the universe loved me? The revelation changed my life.

I nursed that beginning of a relationship like a tender young seedling in my heart. As I got older, my desires grew and changed, and my understanding of life deepened. But I could not forget the startling reality of my nine-year-old revelation—that the God of the universe loved me. I never again feared going to hell.

That abandoned child's fear was replaced by a new fear—gentler, but more potent. I wanted nothing to damage this tender seedling of love, nothing to come between me and this startling Person I had glimpsed. It was all I really wanted: to know this Person better. He allured and called me. The words were gentle, but they pierced me.

When I was a young woman of twenty-two, I dedicated my life to him in a public service. Trembling, joyful, reckless, I prayed these words: I'll go where you want me to go, dear Lord. I'll do what you want me to do. I'll say what you want me to say, dear Lord. I'll be what you want me to be.

With all my heart, I meant every word.

But time moves on, and I move with it. I have not stood unwavering in that holy and dedicated spot. Rather, it is the opposite. In the years since I made that promise, I have gone through intense periods of questioning God. I have felt anger toward him. I have felt my faith rocked by doubt until I could only hold on to the sides of the boat and pray I would not sink.

I do not know why this is, unless it is that Satan hates my prayer of dedication as much as I love it.

Trying to understand myself, I look for the root of the doubts. These are my conclusions:

1. In the intervening years since that prayer, I have become far more connected to the world outside my small Christian community. The Internet is a huge connector. Work, and the people and lifestyles I come into contact with there, is another.

I read widely and am influenced by the books and articles that I read.

But the most powerful of my connectors are the friendships I have formed, and the real admiration and love I have conceived for people who make no profession of Christianity and may even oppose it. Real flesh-and-blood people will always be more effective than disembodied words.

2. Whatever fuels it, the real source of my doubt comes from within. The doubts are vague and all-encompassing. When I examine them, they have no basis in anything solid or reasonable—and yet they have the power to sway me to my depth. I wonder why this is, and have concluded that the doubts are fed not from an outside source but from some faithless corner of my heart. The reasons for my doubt have changed many times, but it does not really matter what those reasons are. Any reason, however groundless, would have the capability to cause me to stop and reconsider my faith. This doubt is a part of my fallen nature. It is my rebellion, my blindness, my self-thinking pride, my inability to comprehend God.

3. I am gullible. I tend to believe what people tell me. When people tell me conflicting things, I have a problem. Enough said.

4. Hell is still my biggest problem. I no longer fear it, but I grapple with the idea of it. This biblical concept of a lost humanity headed toward a doomed eternity is the one part of my faith I do not like.

5. I have felt myself ashamed of my faith. I have been told I am narrow-minded, nonintellectual, old-fashioned. These things sting.

I wish that the Bible's teachings would be less harsh, less single-minded, and more pleasing to other people. I wish that there wasn't found in its pages such an inflexibility of right and wrong. I wish that I could read the Bible and, reading it, still happily believe that everyone, regardless of belief system or moral choice, is headed for the same happy hunting ground. It would be more pleasant. So much easier. No offense involved.

I look with envy at these other people—the ones who have no bulky Bible beliefs to weigh them down. It would be nice, I think, to be "normal" like them. Nice to live without this deep sense of responsibility toward humanity. Nice to live in the moment, with no thought of eternity. Nice to live without the obligation of sharing my faith. It would be pleasant to align myself with the "in" crowd, to choose my own beliefs and make them acceptable, intellectual, and easy. How fun it would be, I tell myself, to be able to live that way.

And the writing that is so important to me. Too bad the only thing I am really passionate about is Jesus. It would be easier to write about something else.

But who am I kidding? If I didn't have Jesus stuck in my head, my life wouldn't be easier. It would only be lonelier. Someone once said to me, "We are all lonely," and I thought, "But I'm not." Yes, sometimes I have felt alienated and vastly different from other people. But at times like this, I talk to God and know that he understands me in a way no one else can. His hands formed me, and he is my Friend. I am never lonely, because he is with me.

Maybe, if I didn't have Jesus, I could choose easier beliefs, but it's more likely that I wouldn't know what to believe. Believing all things, I would end by believing nothing.

Maybe, if Jesus wasn't stuck in my head, I could write books that were popular and acceptable. But I think I would not. I think I would still be a scared little girl, lying in a bed and unable to handle my world. Jesus is my passion and my courage. He makes my life worth living. He gives me something to write about.

Maybe, if I didn't have Jesus, I would be free from this burdening responsibility toward humanity. But I would also have to live without this deep love for people that I know comes from him. I would have to live without the words he speaks to me in the early mornings, live without the joy that fulfills my longings, live without his love that is close as a wedding band around my heart.

I would give up everything—every home, every friend, every dream—in order to keep this one friendship with Jesus that began when I was a scared nine-year-old girl.

Jesus told a little story about a field one time. I know exactly what he meant by it. "The kingdom of heaven is like treasure hidden in a field. When a man found it, he hid it again, and then in his joy went and sold all he had and bought that field" (Matthew 13:44 NIV).

This is me. It doesn't matter how the doubts rock me, or how vicious they are. In the end, I must come to Jesus.

He is my everything. He is my field.

Lucinda

~ *34* ~

The Circle of Love

MARIE COBLENTZ

*B*y the time this is printed, our winter, or most of it, will be gone. We'll be thinking of seed catalogs, weedless gardens, and pretty flower beds. Another necessity will probably be getting out to get some neglected exercise. When the snow blows and the winds howl, we tend to sit around the sewing machine and watch it blow. The pounds have a way of slowly piling on us.

A while back, I heard a minister tell a story of how he was talking to a friend. His friend told him his picture of us Plain people. He said that we have God in the home, community, and unity. I pray we can live our lives in such a way that this is true.

I had a real taste of this a while back when a group of us women were together for the day at a friend's house for her birthday. This is a group that, as young folks, were mostly in the same church district. But when we got married, we all went in somewhat different directions. Some we didn't see or hear from for a long time. One is widowed with a few children still at home. One has a child with special needs.

Well, as we age and our children fly out of the nest, we get a longing for unity again. So this day when we got together was a special day. I called it a "circle of love." One of the quilts I had recently quilted for a lady had something drastically go wrong. And yes, every stitch had to be ripped out! So when I got ready to go to this gathering of friends, I put the quilt in a bag to take along with me to work on during our day together. I put in a few extra seam rippers (just in case).

When I got my quilt out, I was rewarded with a pity party from the other women in the group. Soon all the seam rippers were being put to good use! Now picture this: seven women sitting in a circle, ripping and talking. Over the course of the day, the circle got tighter and smaller as some of us had to leave, one by one, until finally there was room for only two. Then all of a sudden we were done. Our circle of love was completed for this day. What a good feeling to have such precious friends. This is one form of unity.

One day last summer, a different group gathered. This group was made up of old school buddies. We sat around a campfire and roasted hotdogs and made s'mores while we reminisced about bygone school days. Oh, what a joyful day we had!

As we get older, our thoughts turn more and more to the reality that this will someday come to an end. May we all be ready to meet our Savior. "I will greatly rejoice in the LORD . . . for he hath clothed me with the garments of salvation, he hath covered me with the robe of righteousness" (Isaiah 61:10 KJV).

Marie

~ *35* ~

Counseling Your
Own Heart

LAUREN STOLZFOOS

*J*he world whispered cold a few days before Christmas. At
a time when it seemed that everyone else was rejoicing in
the love of family and friends, I felt lost. Pulling my coat tighter
from the wind, ignoring the Christmas jingles and merrymak-
ers, I walked slowly in the falling snow.

Christmas did not feel like Christmas that year. My nose and
my heart were numb, and every lit tree and every carol was a
reminder to me that my life was not right.

Maybe this is you right now. You dread the holidays because of a loss, a complicated new season of life, or a sad turn of
events. The questions, the pain, the unfulfilled longings shout
loudly, demanding to be answered. There is no silent night for
your heart this winter.

Perhaps you are serving in the mission field, and the heat
and the new culture make you want to board every plane you
see flying overhead (oh yeah, I've been there). Or maybe you

are a new bride in a new community, and a trip home isn't going to happen; it's the first Christmas you ever spent away from your family. You feel misplaced, uprooted. Or maybe you have to go home to your family, and you dread it. It's no Hallmark card around your family Christmas table. Maybe you have just experienced a tremendous, heart-shattering loss and the idea of entering the holidays is paralyzing. It hurts too much to even think about the obligatory festivities.

I don't know your situation, but I do know that holidays have a way of amplifying the pain in one's life. It can seem as if everyone is happy but you. Comparison is the thief of joy. Living in a loss of any kind gives you the (false!) perspective that everyone has someone and everyone has it better. Don't fall into comparing. Let go of the expectations ("This is how it always has been, and this is how it always must be!") and the sense of entitlement ("I deserve a perfect life with a perfect holiday, just how I want it!").

The Psalms are full of David counseling his heart. I love the thought of talking to my heart, telling it a thing or two: "Soul, let's get back on track." Or as David said, "Why are you cast down, O my soul, and why are you in turmoil within me? Hope in God; for I shall again praise him, my salvation" (Psalm 42:5 ESV). The holidays offer many opportunities for counseling our hearts—for guarding them from comparison and entitlement and guiding them into truth and thankfulness.

In the ebb and flow of life, there will be happy holidays and sad holidays. I'm so sorry if you are in a sad holiday this winter. But please know that it is okay for this holiday to be shaded darker than the others in your life. Allow it to bring you closer to Jesus, for you to feel the need of his healing deeper than you have ever felt it before.

Years ago, right before the holidays, my father left our family. It was the worst holiday season ever. I spent Thanksgiving dinner crying, brokenhearted, in a dark room. I didn't eat a thing that day. I was sure I would never eat again.

But God and time brought perspective. I did eat again—and I have had many, many happy Thanksgivings since that horrible holiday. The sadness of yesterday brings new thankfulness for the joy of today.

The painful holidays—the one where the friends were gone and the settings were new and the family strewn—are the ones that brought me to my knees the longest, the hardest. The holiday when I felt as though I were walking around with a heart in two pieces is the one I look back on and realize: it was then that I felt Jesus to be closest. It was that holiday that the story of his coming to earth was the most meaningful. Because isn't it when we feel that we need saving the most that we are most thankful for salvation?

If you are in a shaded and dark holiday this year, I cry with you and hold you close. It's sad to be sad during the holidays. But please remember: it will not be like this forever. This too shall pass. There will be happier days ahead. Walk in this changing situation knowing the tears will turn to smiles again, the beautiful Christmas happiness will return. I promise.

Now my holidays are bright (although I still can't listen to "I'll Be Home for Christmas" without tearing up). Holidays are about wrapping a bow around a green tractor for my little boy, stealing a kiss from my husband under the mistletoe, and enjoying time with family and close friends. It's a good season, a season of rest and joy. I know that it's a gift, this season of joy, and I hold it close—cradle it softly in my hands, knowing how fragile it is. It can all change in a blink, a flash.

Even while I cradle this gift of joy, I cry with my friends whose holidays look dark, painful, unsettling this year. I pray for my friend who has an empty crib, a young wife who reaches to find her husband missing in the night, a friend who watches lovers all around her and silently wonders if she will ever have a family of her own. I cry with my friend who is lonely in a new community, feeling misplaced and forgotten. Together we are Tiny Tims looking into the window of plenty and joy with our fingers numb and our tummies hollow, wishing for something to make the ache go away.

That something is Jesus. He is the true meaning behind the holidays, and he is the only reason we can have hope when all seems dark during them. He alone will fill us with good things. Spend lots of time with Jesus to keep yourself grounded and to gain fresh perspective on what he is doing in your life this holiday.

And be gentle—very gentle—with yourself.

Being in a new setting—whether physically or emotionally—is a vulnerable, scary place. The holidays have a way of making the vulnerable heart even more raw and tender. Be prepared for unexpected pain—and unexpected joy. Let the tears flow, and don't try to pretend everything is okay. But don't fall into despair. God is in the healing business. He will heal. Joy is around the corner. Redemption is nigh.

And isn't that what Christmas is all about? Redemption. Jesus came to redeem; that's his chief business. He wants to take the hard things of life and make them into something beautiful. He wants to take your hard holiday and turn it into something beautiful. Allow him to do his work.

Mary, the mother of Jesus, found herself in the center of the Christmas story in a greatly changing world. In many ways, her life was being painted in a swirl of unexpected, complicated colors. Her response to her changing circumstances is in Luke 1. She says, "My soul glorifies the Lord and my spirit rejoices in God my Savior" (Luke 1:46-47 NIV). She also sings, "He has filled the hungry with good things" (Luke 1:53 NIV). He does fill us with good things.

I pray your life will be full of good things, even in the loss, the uprooting, and the disappointments. Keep your heart open and tender to the good things he will bring your way.

Allow him to bring you joy during the holidays. I remember how a week before Christmas, after my dad left, I hadn't smiled for days. My heart was in so much pain. Someone said something funny, and I laughed. First a smile, and then a belly laugh. It actually hurt to smile, but it was healing. I felt a twinge of guilt from laughing at a time of such loss, but I realized God was giving me a gift through that funny word. It was a reprieve from the sadness, no matter how fleeting. Allow God to give you joy. Keep your heart open for it, for pain increases the heart's capacity to receive joy.

This is your beautiful story, even if the paints on the canvas right now are strong strokes of gray and black. The shaded parts will only make the bright parts that much more glorious. The darkness will bring new meaning to the light. One day you will look back on this sad and unsettling time and say, "Thank you and amen."

Weary heart, rejoice. Your redemption is nigh.

Lauren

36

Rebuilding from the Shambles of Shame

SAMANTHA TRENKAMP

I love old, decrepit houses. They are so full of history and nostalgia. Yet people often just leave them to waste away, and only those in dire need would abide under such roofs. We look at these places and think, What a shame! But if someone had taken the time to care for such a house long ago, there would still be life within those walls.

Not long ago, I had to face the fact that I had made an utter fool of myself over a two-and-half-year period. I had chased after things that were never meant to be mine—and it wasn't a private thing, either. So when I came to my senses, I had to confront those closest to me about how painfully misguided I had been.

Although my mom's response may sound harsh, the greatest comfort came from her. "I feel like such a fool!" I told her.

"Well," she said, "that's just life. Sometimes we will make fools of ourselves."

That was exactly what I needed to hear! I was encouraged to know that millions of other people have made ridiculous mistakes, have also made fools of themselves, and have had to bear the shame. But life goes on.

Yes, I may have tripped and fallen flat, but I don't have to stay that way! Satan wants us to stay in the mire. At every opportunity, he will strive to remind us of all the blunders we have made. Or maybe you are carrying a burden of another kind. Maybe the shame you feel doomed to live with is the result of others' actions. The sense of shame that comes from having been used and abused, mishandled and cast aside. Maybe you didn't fall in the mud; maybe you were thrown there.

Whether the mud stains of shame have been self-inflicted or imposed by others, we can feel as if we've been battered and bruised. Either way, we can make a choice. We have two options. We can stay stretched out on the ground with our hands over our head, afraid to face the world again and wallowing in self-pity. Or we can determine to not let the shame of our fall take away the glory that God desires to have through our lives in Christ Jesus. We can choose to not allow the enemy to snatch away the desire to live our lives fully.

Having been made in the image of God, we represent to the world just what he looks like. If we are always full of sorrow and shame, then that is the image the world will register. Who wants to commit to a life like that? The world has enough trouble of its own. We are to be the light of the world! We are supposed to bear the fruit of the Spirit as we live out days of joy and love and kindness and peace.

But how do we gain the courage to get back up again? To go back and start repairing those crumbled walls? To rise up and see glory in the midst of the shame?

If every inventor had given in to the destructive feelings of shame, nothing would have ever gotten off the ground. Inventors endure many failures and embarrassing endeavors before something of worth is produced. They face rejection, criticism, and mocking, but they keep at it because they know it will be worth it in the end.

Bearing shame is no different than any other trial we face as we grow into the stature of Christ. Just as anger, temptation, and pride can all destroy us from the inside out, we can surrender our failures to God, and he can turn those things around. Only he can bring grace, glory, life, and peace to our hearts. God always has a flip side to a situation.

Shame can also be a blessing in disguise. It can cause our hearts to be stirred to realize a greater need of the Holy Spirit within us. We feel shame because of sin in our lives, and so we seek God. We feel shame because of things that have happened to us, through no fault of our own, and so we must go to the Lord for healing and affirmation.

The ugly becomes beautiful, the wound gives way to health, the shame gives birth to life lived in sweet abandon to a loving Father. Shame can become yet another tool to teach us to lean hard on God.

This process is not something we can just determine to do. We must give it all to the Lord and trust him to make everything new. We don't have to live with shame.

Pray for courage to put your hand in God's and to take the journey up those rickety steps. Pray as you back through that lopsided doorway and work your way with him through each of those rooms that are all paint-peeled and caving in.

Waste no more time in letting the rain seep in, damaging more and more of the foundation. Get in there and start remodeling! Rebuild the old wasted places on the firm corner-stone of our Savior.

Start rebuilding the beauty of who you are created to be.

There is no shame in that.

Samantha

37

Jesus, Who Lives
in the Mud

LUCINDA J. MILLER

A few days before Easter, I stride in boots down the
gravel road that runs past our house, looking back at
heel prints left in soft dirt. Water and half-melted snow pool
in ditches. I scoop up a handful of soggy gravel and smell it.
But the peculiar scent of earthy spring is not in the gravel. In
the fields, I think. Soon. I twist my boot on its heel, grinding
it into mud and loving it. Easter will be here soon. And Jesus
lives in mud.

A few evenings earlier, thanks to a spring snowstorm and
canceled plans, all eight of us are home and in one place. This
rarely happens. My two sisters spread fabric down the center
of the living room floor to cut out dress pieces for sewing. My
brothers and I sprawl on the couches and chairs, each in our
separate world of computer or Kindle or old-fashioned book.

"Righteous people don't need Jesus to get to God," I an-
nounce into the center of my family.

My siblings and parents jerk up and look at me. In my evangelical Christian family, such a statement is scandalous.

"It's true," I say. "Jesus said, 'I have not come to call the righteous, but sinners to repentance'" (Luke 5:32 NIV).

They argue with me. "You're taking that verse out of context."

"No, I'm not," I retort. "That's what it says. Righteous people don't need Jesus."

"But *nobody* is righteous."

"But some people think they're righteous."

Understanding lights one sister's eyes. "She's talking about people like the Pharisees."

"See? *She* understands what I mean," I say.

They are suspicious. "So you're just saying that some people are self-righteous and think they don't need Jesus?"

"I'm saying that some people think they don't need Jesus, and so they don't need him."

My brother is disgusted. "Way to make something simple into something complicated."

But I know that, for myself, I am making something complicated into something simple.

I used to be confused by Jesus, because I viewed him as a sort of Holy Wizard pointing to heaven: "Believe in me, or be damned." The little phrases found on the back of every evangelical tract—"Ask Jesus into your heart"; "Accept Christ as your personal Savior"—I unconsciously thought of as magical incantations. Utter these words in this order and—voilà!—you're saved.

In fact, Jesus seemed to me the height of unfairness. What about the people who hadn't heard, or those who were deeply rooted in other religions? Were they to be damned because of where they were born?

But that was before I began to observe this whole sodden mass of humanity, before I began to identify with us and to realize the sorry state we are in. Whatever our race, nationality, financial status, or religion, we are driven by a basic selfishness. Not one of us lives up to our own idea of what is good. We are covered in sorrow.

We have no need of a Holy Wizard to damn us. We are already damned.

* * *

I met Vienna at a recent bridal shower. She wore a sheer black top, a short, glittery mauve skirt, and black hose. She had a small silver ring in her nose and tiny silver studs on either side of her eyes, which were made up in heavy black to appear slanted, like a cat's eyes. She told me she wore heavy makeup to cover the scars of a face that had been badly mauled. She was friendly, vivacious, intelligent.

I met Vienna's boyfriend, also, before the shower. He asked me questions about being a Mennonite and told me that he also had a Christian background. "I might be living in sin now," he said, "but I've heard that if you pray, even on your deathbed, you'll be okay."

He explained to me that living the sort of good life the Bible talked about was just too hard in this modern world—foreign, like living on Mars—and asked if I understood.

I did.

But Vienna, who made no profession of Christianity, I liked better. About halfway through the event, she asked if I would ever be interested in getting a body piercing.

"No," I said.

"But would you be interested in knowing why someone else might do it?"

"Oh yes."

So she told me why she did it—to identify with a subculture, something outside the mainstream. She told me how each of her piercings was significant, that they were a sort of sacrifice given for loved ones who had died and a way of connecting to these loved ones, whose spirits were in the stars. I understood. My Mennonite way of dress is also significant.

There was alcohol available at the shower. Some drank a glass or two. Vienna drank many. By the end of the evening she had lost her intelligence and become silly, emotional, and random. She told me all about her Flemish Giant rabbit, which stood as high as a Shetland sheepdog. She lay on her back with her legs in the air to show how it looked when it wanted to have its belly scratched, and demonstrated its "murrs" and its guttural noises repeatedly. Out on the porch, she told me, with feeling, "I love you. I will love you for the rest of my life." I just stood there while she waited and her eyes got large. After a while she said something about a squirrel, laughed, and went into the house.

Someone turned on the television. Rioting in the city. Our host, a gentle young mother of two, walked up to the screen and pointed it away from herself. "I'll be fine, as long as I don't have to look at that."

I think of the gentle host, and Vienna with her body piercings and her hurts from the past, and the boyfriend, and the rioters on the television, and myself. I think of us as one large, breathing mass of humanity. We struggle for good; we are surrounded, crushed in, and attracted by evil. They—the good and the evil—are two in us, warring, and we wonder if the good ever wins, or if it is always the evil.

We are one with the young man who stares down depression, one with the starving black-eyed baby who will not stop crying, one with the girl-child sold into prostitution. We are one with the cowering woman beaten into submission, and one with the gray-eyed maniac who beats her. This is Vienna. This is me. And this is Jesus, who lives in the mud.

* * *

I realize now that Jesus is not a Holy Wizard, come down to save the people born into the right time and the right place and the right religion. He is not a magical incantation uttered from a book. He is not three simple steps to salvation. Jesus is someone who stepped into a need greater than the world and said, "I have a solution."

The righteous, or those who think they are righteous, will not see a need for Jesus. But Jesus never came for the righteous people.

He came for those who are succumbing to evil and don't know how to stop. He came for those who long for God and don't know how to reach him. He came for those who are sick to death of their own sin and can find no religion to help them conquer it. He came to be the hope in the young man's eye, the future of the starving child, the avenger of the prostituted girl, the comfort of the cowering woman, the regeneration of the wife beater.

This is Jesus, who sees no sin too great, no hurt too deep. Jesus, who transforms lives, breaks iron chains, casts demons down to the depths of hell. Jesus, who fulfills my God-longing and opens the doorway to spiritual life.

This is Jesus, who is everything: my alcohol, my sports craze, my lover, my drug.

This is Jesus, who lives in mud.

Lucinda

Notes

A Side of Conversation

Page 42 One website defines the practice: Camila Loew, "What Is Sobremesa," Sobremesa, February 3, 2104, https://sobremesa.life/blog/2014/2/3/what-is-sobremesa.

Page 42 "The shared meal elevates eating": Michael Pollan, *In Defense of Food: An Eater's Manifesto* (New York: Penguin, 2008), 192.

The Lord Is My Rock

Page 85 "Believing that God rules all": Charles H. Spurgeon, "Morning, August 5," in *The Devotional Classics of C. H. Spurgeon: Morning and Evening 1 and 2* (Lafayette, IN: Sovereign Grace Publishers, 1990).

Page 85 "The greatest good": Joni Eereckson Tada and Steven Estes, *When God Weeps: Why Our Sufferings Matter to the Almighty* (Grand Rapids: Zondervan, 1997), 109.

Season of Doubt

Page 107 "Lives lie bleakly frozen": Janice Etter, "Choose Life," *The Vindicator* (Old German Baptist Brethren publication), 2014.

The Lord Is My Sufficiency

Page 201 "On my own, I do not have": Ann Voskamp, *One Thousand Gifts: A Dare to Live Fully Right Where You Are* (Grand Rapids: Zondervan, 2010), 68.

The Authors

Danielle Beiler ("When You Put Your Money in God's Bank") is a teacher whose life is rich and varied and keeps her consciously dependent on Jesus. When she has time for something other than teaching, she loves to read, travel, and spend time with her nieces and nephews. She is a member of a Biblical Mennonite Alliance Church in Gap, Pennsylvania.

Martha Beiler ("Should You Happen to Stop By") is an Old Order Amish woman who lives in Perry County, Pennsylvania. She is a busy mother of seven, and each new day is an adventure on the farm. She enjoys writing when she gets a chance, loves eating chocolate, and is thankful to be a mom with a dear husband by her side.

Linda Byler ("On Appreciative Overnight Guests" and "Bone Opp-a-Deet!") is the author of four bestselling fiction series, all set in the Amish world: Hester's Hunt for Home, Lancaster Burning, Sadie's Montana, and Lizzie Searches for Love. In addition, Byler has written four Christmas romances. Linda is Old Order Amish and is well known within the Amish community as a columnist for *The Connection*. She and her husband have seven children and twenty-five grandchildren.

Marie Coblentz ("The Horse That Wouldn't Budge" and "The Circle of Love") has been married to Marvin Coblentz for forty-five years. Marvin is a bishop in the Old Order Amish church. They live in Holmes County, Ohio, and they both sew for a living, for retailers and wholesalers. Marie and Marvin have seven children and thirty-one grandchildren.

Lovina Eicher ("The Home Place") is an Old Order Amish writer, cook, wife, and mother of eight. She writes a syndicated newspaper column called Lovina's Amish Kitchen, which appears in newspapers across the United States. She is the coauthor of three cookbooks, and her newest cookbook, *The Essential Amish Cookbook*, was published by Herald Press in 2017.

Barbara Fisher ("Remains of the Doll") is an Amish woman in her seventies. She has been married to Gideon A. Fisher since 1965. Their eleven children all flew the nest, so they moved off the farm sixteen years ago. They still enjoy the children and grandchildren when they come to visit.

Catherine Gascho ("The Angels' Charge") is the mother of six ambitious children ages one to fourteen. She and her husband both think there's nothing as cozy as snuggling down with a book on a dark rainy evening or a cold wintry evening before a blazing fire. They are Mennonites living in Missouri.

Sherry Gore ("Zippy") is the author of seven books, including *Simply Delicious Amish Cooking*; *Me, Myself, and Pie*; and *The Plain Choice*. The National Geographic Channel featured Gore in their documentary series *Amish: Out of Order*, and she has appeared on *NBC Daytime*, the *Today Show*, *Mr. Food Test Kitchen*, and more. Sherry, who is Beachy Amish, is a resident of Sarasota, Florida, and speaks widely on topics such as cooking, living after loss, and discovering one's true identity in Christ.

Bethany Hege ("White Space") lives in rural northern Minnesota with her husband, her dog, and a growing population of cats. She enjoys traveling, finding a good coffee shop, and everyday life at home. She attends Noahwood Chapel, which is part of Midwest Mennonite Fellowship.

Vicki Kauffman ("A Life That Says Welcome") loves reading, playing with her watercolors, and hosting friends. She is passionate about women living vibrantly and abundantly. She attends Followers of Jesus at Thomaston and occasionally spills her heart on writtendownbigblog.wordpress.com.

Stephanie J. Leinbach ("Seized by Grace") is a member of a Pilgrim Mennonite church and lives in the mountains of central Pennsylvania with her husband, Linford, and four children. Three more children dwell in the arms of Jesus; she writes about them in *Light My Candle: Prayers in the Darkness of Miscarriage*. You can contact Stephanie at www.stephaniejleinbach.com.

Lucinda J. Miller ("I Would Sell Everything and Buy a Field" and "Jesus, Who Lives in the Mud") is a writer, teacher, blogger, and member of a conservative Mennonite community in Wisconsin. She teaches elementary school at the Sheldon Mennonite Church, and her book *Anything but Simple: My Life as a Mennonite* (Herald Press, 2017) describes her life. Connect with her at www.lucindajmiller.com.

DeLora Neuschwander ("Where Your Soul Belongs") is a writer and musician currently residing in Brooklyn, New York. She is a member of Living Water Mennonite Church, which is affiliated with the Biblical Mennonite Alliance.

Holli Nisly ("Holli's House") is a married Mennonite woman in her twenties who currently resides in Kansas. She is learning that if she wants to be a vibrant part of her church, community, and marriage, she must first be a vibrant individual. To that end she is pursuing some of her talents and dreams, which include writing and singing.

Sara Nolt ("An Unforgettable Lesson in Hospitality"; "Heaven Our Home"; and "Overcoming Inferiority") is married to John and is the mother of three children. She attends Charity Christian Fellowship in Pennsylvania. Nolt spent seven years in West Africa, an experience that greatly influenced her life and writings. Find more from Sara on her blog, dewdropsofeternaljoy.blogspot.com.

Sheila Petre ("Season of Doubt" and "The Way of a Man") lives with her husband, Michael, and their seven children, born between 2007 and 2017, in south central Pennsylvania. They are members of the Washington-Franklin County Mennonite Conference. Sheila's collection of motherhood-related tales, *Thirty Little Fingers*, was published in 2017.

Katie Shrock ("God's Protecting Hand") and her husband, Jethro, and four children live in Garrison, Montana, nestled between the banks of the Little Blackfoot River and what is said to be the shortest state highway in the United States—Highway 10. Their church is a part of the Mennonite Christian Fellowship.

Rae Schrock ("Love Begins in the Kitchen"; "A Side of Conversation"; and "The Lord Is My Sufficiency") is a native of beautiful East Tennessee, where she grew up loving the wildness of the mountains and rivers near her home. She is a transplant to southern Virginia, where she works part-time as an RN at a crisis pregnancy center and full-time as chief editor of *Daughters of Promise* magazine. In her free time you'll find her reading in her hammock, dabbling in freelance design, and enjoying good conversation over a mug of coffee.

Denise Shank ("The Perfect Mother-in-Law") is the pen name of a conservative Mennonite author from the East Coast. She is married to a kind man, and they have six delightful children.

Gertrude Slabach ("Open House" and "Stories Rustling in the Branches") is a mom to six adult children, a mother-in-law, and sometimes a foster mom. She is married to Dave, who is associate pastor of Faith Mennonite Church (Mountain Valley Mennonite Churches) in Southside, Virginia. She is a nurse, a speaker, and a writer, and she blogs about faith, family, and food at mywindowsill.com.

Dorcas Smucker ("Still Ourselves—Just a Lot More") is a mother of six and a Mennonite minister's wife. She is the author of numerous books, including *Ordinary Days*; *Upstairs the Peasants Are Revolting*; *Downstairs the Queen Is Knitting*; and *Tea and Trouble Brewing*. In addition to blogging and speaking to various groups, Smucker also writes a column for *The Register-Guard* in Eugene, Oregon. She resides in Harrisburg, Oregon.

Lauren Stolzfoos ("Counseling Your Own Heart") lives in Lancaster, Pennsylvania, with her husband, Delmar, and two children, Hudson and Luke. They attend West End Mennonite Fellowship.

Samantha Trenkamp ("Rebuilding from the Shambles of Shame") hails from the rolling hills of East Tennessee, where she is a member of Wellspring Mennonite Church. She lives with her parents and two brothers. A devoted scribbler and book lover, she enjoys being involved in ministry, spending quality time with friends, teaching, kayaking, hiking, and engaging in stimulating discussions about the Bible.

Mary Troyer ("Stretched") and her husband belong to the Beachy Amish Church and moved to Plummer, Idaho, in May 2017 from Sarasota, Florida. They have three sons, one daughter, and nineteen grandchildren spread between Idaho, Wisconsin, and Virginia.

Melissa Troyer ("The Kingdom Here in Our Arms") is a freelance writer, busy mother of four delightful children, and wife to the man of her dreams. She and her family currently live in North Carolina and are in the middle of remodeling a farmhouse, juggling homeschooling, and being part of Cleveland Believers' Fellowship. She blogs at danilissa.wordpress.com.

Mae Unruh ("Ground-Laid Eggs") is a retired LPN and a member of the Church of God in Christ, Mennonite, in Kansas. She is the youngest of seven siblings. She has been active in family and church genealogy and china painting, and she collects books, stories, poems, and other interesting articles. She has traveled throughout the United States, Canada, Mexico, Europe, and the Middle East.

Ervina Yoder ("The Lord Is My Rock") is a twentysomething who, five years ago, traded her globe-trotting single life for the adventure of marriage and motherhood. She grew up Mennonite in Lancaster County, Pennsylvania, and recently moved to Ohio with her husband and two adorable kids.

Rhoda Yoder ("My Father's Amish Home") and her husband, Daniel, built their home in the rolling hills of southern Illinois, where they revel in family, friends, sunsets, and the three sweetest grandbabies ever. Her hobbies include writing, reading, flower gardening, cake decorating, and creative cooking. Rhoda and Daniel are members of the New Order Amish Church in Ava, Illinois.

The Editor

Lorilee Craker is the author of fifteen books, including *Money Secrets of the Amish*; *Anne of Green Gables, My Daughter, and Me*; *My Journey to Heaven* with Marv Besteman; and the *New York Times* bestseller *Through the Storm* with Lynne Spears. Connect with her at LorileeCraker.com and on Instagram @thebooksellersdaughter.

DAUGHTERS *of* PROMISE

a quarterly magazine for Christian women, from an Anabaptist perspective.

Theme verse

"And if you belong to Christ, then you are Abraham's descendants, heirs according to the promise." Gal. 3:29

ISSUES ARE PRODUCED QUARTERLY AND FEATURE:

- » 112+ pages, offset printed on uncoated paper
- » book-bound, coffee-table presentation
- » essays, DIY projects, recipes, and interviews to equip women for wholly healthy living as daughters of God & heirs through Christ
- » original writing, artwork, and photography reflecting conservative Anabaptist values

Contact

FACEBOOK: Daughters of Promise
BLOG: daughters-of-promise.org/blog
INSTAGRAM: @daughtersofpromise
EMAIL: hello@daughters-of-promise.org

WWW.DAUGHTERS-OF-PROMISE.ORG

Ladies' JOURNAL

A bimonthly magazine of **INSPIRATION** and encouragement by women of faith for *all ages.*

CPSIA information can be obtained
at www.ICGtesting.com
Printed in the USA
BVHW03*1813080818
523949BV00004B/12/P